U.K
LOW CHOLESTEROL
COOKBOOK

Super tasty heart Healthy Recipes to lower your high
cholesterol includes 30 Day meal plan for quick relief

Jeffery F. Maurer

Jeffery F. Maurer

TABLE OF CONTENT

INTRODUCTION

I had high cholesterol for many years, and it was beginning to take a toll on my health. My doctor warned me that I might be in danger of heart disease and other significant health issues if I didn't make some lifestyle adjustments.

Therefore, I decided to take matters into my own hands and reduce my cholesterol levels by changing my diet (as instructed by my doctor). I began by removing processed items from my diet and substituting more whole, unprocessed foods, such as fruits, vegetables, nuts, and seeds. Also, I stopped eating fried dishes, red meat, and other things high in saturated fat.

My diet initially felt somewhat limiting, but I quickly adapted to it and even started to enjoy some of the new foods I was eating. I also began to include consistent exercise in my daily life. I began by just strolling, then worked up to jogging. I expanded my practice by including some mild yoga and strength training.

My cholesterol levels changed after six months of following a healthy diet and exercising frequently. My LDL cholesterol also decreased, going from 152 to 117, and my total cholesterol went from 216 to 177. I was overjoyed with my outcomes and had never felt more energized. I kept up my healthy habits and was successful in maintaining healthy cholesterol levels.

I'm really happy that my diet and exercise alone were enough to lower my cholesterol. I've changed my lifestyle for a few years now, and I'm still reaping the Benefits. I'm happier and more active than I've ever been right now. I am proof that lowering cholesterol levels may be accomplished only through diet and exercise.

This book's objective is not to ramble on about the risks of cholesterol. Instead, it's about laying out a plan that combines doable fitness objectives and simple, delectable foods.

It is a strategy to get your low-cholesterol lifestyle off the ground.

Let's get started.

CHAPTER 1

INTRODUCTION TO CHOLESTEROL

Everyone's body contains cholesterol, a fatty molecule. In order for several of our organs, including the heart and brain, to operate, they actually need cholesterol. It circulates in the bloodstream throughout the body and is metabolized by the liver. It isn't a problem at the moment. When we have too much cholesterol, we have a problem. Plaque, which is essentially just cholesterol that the body stores in a blood artery and is covered over with a protective coating, can attach itself to the walls of our blood vessels. Yet, there are a number of issues with that. One is that a blood vessel may become blocked if the plaque accumulates to that point. The blood supply to vital organs including the heart and brain may be restricted as a result. If the covering is damaged and the cholesterol is released back into the bloodstream, another issue arises. In an effort to get the cholesterol back under control, the body responds by sending substances that aid in blood clotting, which can result in a blood clot. Heart attacks occur when a blood clot in the heart blocks an artery. It is a stroke if it occurs in the brain.

THE TRUTH BEHIND THE CAUSE OF HIGH CHOLESTEROL

According to television commercials, cholesterol is brought on by both inherited and dietary causes. The likelihood that you will have high cholesterol rises if your parents or grandparents did. One thing that doctors are unsure of right now is whether the heightened risk is totally inherited or whether those who eat poorly tend to do the same, suggesting that even inherited risk may still be partially influenced by food. What is certain is that nutrition has a significant impact on cholesterol levels. Saturated fats are the main offender in our diets. Sadly, many of the foods we enjoy eating—such as fatty meats, fried foods, high-fat dairy items like whole milk, cream, and cheese made from whole milk, as well as professionally produced baked goods—are rich in saturated fats. We'll look at some substitutes that are lower in saturated fats but still tasty when we get into the recipes in this book.

THE GOOD AND BAD CHOLESTEROL

Your doctor looks for a few different things when he does a blood test to assess your cholesterol levels. These are cholesterol's subcomponents, yet they have quite different health effects. Low-density lipoproteins (LDL), high-density lipoproteins (HDL), and triglycerides are the three main ones that are most frequently tested for. The concentrations of these cholesterol-related substances are expressed in milligrammes per deciliter of blood, or mg/dl. Let's quickly review each of them.

The term "bad cholesterol" is frequently used to describe LDL. It is a portion of your overall cholesterol that is most responsible for clogging your arteries. The risk of a blockage or blood clot increases when LDL binds to the arterial wall because the inflammation it generates encourages additional cholesterol to be deposited there. The main factor contributing to an increase in LDL is consuming foods high in saturated fats.

Despite ongoing debate over the LDL risk threshold, everyone agrees that anything over 200 mg/dl is harmful. Some medical professionals think that even amounts over 100 mg/dl may increase your risk of heart attack and stroke depending on the source and any additional risk factors you may have, such as smoking and being overweight.

Usually referred to as "good cholesterol," HDL. The body uses HDL to assist eliminate the cholesterol buildup in the arteries. A high HDL level suggests that your risk of having a heart attack is generally low. Men should have HDL levels of at least 40 mg/dl, and women should have levels of at least 50 mg/dl. The good news is that raising your

HDL levels tends to follow actions that lower your LDL levels. And increasing healthy fat in your diet can increase HDL levels. Such sources include the oils found in nuts and soybeans, fatty seafood like tuna and salmon, and olive and canola oils. Some studies even contend that consuming alcohol in moderation will increase HDL levels.

Triglycerides are the third important factor in a routine cholesterol screening. Triglycerides, like LDL, can contribute to an accumulation of deposits in the arteries. They are also influenced by a diet rich in saturated fats, just like LDL. Triglyceride levels should be less than 150 mg/dl, according to recommendations. It's definitely crucial to mention that some medical professionals think the ratio between HDL and LDL is even more significant than the individual figures. So, anything we do to increase HDL or lower LDL has a beneficial impact on that ratio.

CHAPTER 2

WHAT CAN I DO TO REDUCE MY CHOLESTEROL?

(Secret Revealed)

As we've seen, a variety of elements affect your cholesterol and general heart health. Some of them, such as genetics and aging, are beyond our control. Some, though, we do. When it comes down to it, there are three basic things we can do to lower cholesterol. One is medication, which you should discuss with your doctor. Exercise is still another. Regular exercise helps cut cholesterol and lower the risk of heart disease and stroke, according to studies.

Lastly, a person's diet. That's why this book was written, too. There are a few dietary changes we can make that will be beneficial. The first step, which is closely related to exercise, is to keep your weight within a healthy range. A known risk factor for heart disease is being overweight.

The second is to reduce the amount of saturated fat in your diet, as was already discussed.

The good news is that it's rather simple to keep track of because nutrition labels are now required to disclose the quantity of saturated fat. Nevertheless, trans fat is also a harmful fat. Trans fatty acids, often known as trans fats, are created when a liquid fat is hydrogenated in order to solidify it at room temperature, as is done when creating margarine. Trans fats are now easier to monitor because they are already indicated on the nutrition labels of packaged goods. Trans fats can be simply calculated by taking the total fat and taking out the saturated fat, monounsaturated fat, and polyunsaturated fat that are provided in the nutritional information, such as in a recipe. The nutritional advice in this book is also accurate in that regard. Any solid fat is generally bad fat. Tropical oils like coconut and palm oil are also bad. One general guideline is to limit your daily intake of saturated and trans fats to no more than 10% of your total calorie intake. The computation is made simpler because 100 calories are contained in each gram of fat. 200 calories, at most, should come from saturated and trans fats if your daily calorie intake is 2,000 (the figure given as a guide on nutrition labels). It translates to a daily maximum of 20 grams of unhealthy fats.

CHAPTER 3

WHAT AM I SUPPOSED TO EAT?

The foods you should consume and the foods you shouldn't eat will be thoroughly examined in this chapter.

FOODS THAT CAN ELEVATE CHOLESTEROL INCLUDE:

1 Saturated fats

2 Meals containing cholesterol

3 trans fats

FOODS THAT TYPICALLY DECREASE CHOLESTEROL INCLUDE:

1 Healthy oils

2 Foods with soluble fibre and whole grains;

3 Foods with omega-3 fatty acids;

1. Saturated Fats

Your cholesterol level is mostly increased by saturated fats. Saturated fats often have a solid consistency at room temperature. Saturated fats fall into a number of categories, and the amount is noted on the nutrition information label on packaged foods. This implies that you have control over the amount of saturated fat you consume. The American Heart Association and other organizations generally advise against consuming more than 20 grammes of saturated fat per day. The recipes in this book will show you where to get the meat cuts and cooking methods that will enable you to accomplish them.

2. Red Meats

The worst meats in terms of saturated fat are frequently regarded as beef, hog, and lamb. Indeed, they frequently serve more than just fish or chicken. But, it really depends on the cut you select and how much they have. Some high-fat beef cuts may have five times as much saturated fat as a lean cut.

a. Poultry Skin

Even though it doesn't have as much red meat, poultry skin has a sizable amount of saturated fat. Compared to a chicken thigh with only the meat, one with the skin contains more than 2 grammes more saturated fat. And in this instance, getting rid of the fat is quite simple—just avoid eating the skin.

C. Whole-Milk Dairy

Making wise decisions can also dramatically lower the quantity of saturated fat in dairy products. Products manufactured with whole milk or cream should not be used. Choose skim milk, low-fat cheeses, sour cream and cream cheese without added fat. replace cream with fat-free evaporated milk.

d. Tropical Oils:

Saturated fats are present in a few of the plant oils in this category. They include cocoa butter, palm, and palm kernel oils. These are normally easy to avoid, but be mindful that some commercial baked goods and processed foods may include them.

3. Trans Fats

Trans-fatty acids are another name for trans fats. They are created by hydrogenating vegetable oil, which is the process of adding hydrogen to it. The fat becomes firmer as a result and is less likely to spoil. Trans fats are still frequently used in commercial baked goods and fried foods, despite growing knowledge of their potential health hazards. Food producers are obligated to disclose the presence of trans fats on nutrition labels. Trans fat serving sizes under 0.5 grammes can be labeled as having 0 grammes of trans fat.

a. Additional hydrogenated oils and margarine

Whenever possible, stay away from margarine and solid shortening made with hydrogenated or partially hydrogenated oils.

In this book, there are a few recipes that employ margarine when the food's texture calls for a solid fat, but in general, use liquid or soft margarine wherever possible. We now almost exclusively "butter" bread and vegetables using butter spray bottles, such as I Can't Believe It's Not Butter! Original Buttery Spray.

b. Commercially prepared fried and baked foods

Understand that hydrogenated oils are frequently used in commercial baked goods by reading ingredient labels. Although awareness has grown and many restaurants now use trans-fat-free frying oils, you should still be cautious of what you are eating.

FOODS CONTAINING CHOLESTEROL

Although your body produces all the cholesterol you require, you can also consume animal products including meat, seafood, eggs, and dairy items. Even though some specialists now concur that dietary cholesterol intake plays a smaller role in elevated cholesterol levels than was previously believed, They continue to encourage people to consume no more than 300 mg of cholesterol per day.

a. Egg Whites

214 mg of cholesterol, or more than two-thirds of the daily recommended maximum, can be found in egg yolk. The good news is

that you may use egg substitutes made mostly from egg whites rather than whole eggs almost anyplace, with the exception of deviled eggs and eggs fried over-easy. Even after cooking some egg in the microwave, cutting it up, and adding mustard and mayonnaise, I've prepared egg salad.

b. Animal Organs

Each serving of beef liver has more than 300 mg of cholesterol, and thequantities in other types of liver and organ meat are comparable. I'll admit that I formerly belonged to the group of folks who enjoyed liver, but I no longer do.

c. SHELLFISH

Each 3-ounce dish of prawn includes more than 130 mg of cholesterol. Moreover, other shellfish frequently rank better than meats and fish. We only eat shellfish occasionally now, despite the fact that I adore it.

d. Healthy Oils

Monounsaturated and polyunsaturated fats are your greatest options when picking a type of fat. By lowering the levels of total and LDL (bad) cholesterol in your blood, it has been demonstrated that these fats reduce your chance of developing heart disease.

e. Monounsaturated Oils

The healthiest fats are monounsaturated ones. As often as you can, swap them out for other fats in your diet. Normally liquid at ambient temperature starts to solidify when placed in the refrigerator.

Examples include avocado fat, olive, canola, and peanut oils. The majority of the recipes in this book call for canola oil for baking and olive oil for both.

f. Polyunsaturated Oils

Polyunsaturated oils are still a far better option than saturated fats and trans fats, while not having quite the advantages of monounsaturated oils. They typically are liquid both at ambient temperature and in the refrigerator, but if kept unrefrigerated for an extended period of time, they might turn rancid.

Safflower, sesame, soy, corn, sunflower, and other seed and nut oils are a few examples.

OMEGA-3 FATTY ACIDS IN MEALS

Omega-3 fatty acids are one type of polyunsaturated fat that may be particularly beneficial for your heart. The risk of coronary artery disease appears to be reduced by omega-3 fatty acids.

1. Fish

Current dietary guidelines typically recommend eating one or two portions of fish each week. Fish, fortunately, works well in a variety of dishes. This book has several fish recipes to get you started. Some, like tuna steaks, are only appropriate for a certain type of fish, but many can be modified to work with any fish you have on hand or can find for a reasonable price.

2. Nuts

To add a little additional omega-3 boost, nuts can be added to a variety of dishes. They are nevertheless a nutritious supplement even though they don't have as much protein as fish. Instead of using bacon bits, think about using them as salad toppers, adding them to baked dishes, or including them in your cereal.

Foods Containing Soluble Fibre And Whole Grains

It has been demonstrated that soluble fibre lowers LDL and total cholesterol without changing HDL (HDL).

1. Oats

Certainly, oats have received the greatest attention for their ability to lower cholesterol. The American Food and Drug Administration was persuaded sufficiently to allow cholesterol-lowering medical claims on packages of oats and oat bran. Oat bran is simple to use in a variety of dishes, such as meat breading mixes and the more popular baked items. Many recipes that use oat bran are presented below. Oatmeal and oat bran producers also offer a tonne of advice on how to increase your consumption of their foods.

2. Barley with beans

There is a substantial quantity of soluble fibre in dried beans and peas. Likewise, cereals like barley.

By serving as the foundation of meals with little to no meat, these products can also assist you in reducing your intake of saturated fats. Here, you'll find a variety of recipes that use them frequently in soups and stews.

3. Whole Grains

Long before the advantages of soluble fibre were fully appreciated, experts were aware that whole grains are healthier than processed grains. When compared to their refined equivalents, whole-grain items like bread, rice, and pasta are frequently an easy move to make. The fantastic news is that some people discover they taste better as well.

4. Veggies And Fruits

Certain fruits and vegetables have soluble fibre levels high enough to be beneficial. Apples, strawberries, oranges, bananas, carrots, corn, cauliflower, and sweet potatoes are the most popular.

CHAPTER 4

HOW CAN WE MAKE OUR DIETS HEALTHIER ?

So what specifically did I do to improve the quality of my diet over my previous eating habits? Below are the general rules I adhered to:

• Make the best possible effort to reduce saturated fats by using wholesome ingredients. Reduce the amount of red meat you eat each week and, if it's on the menu, stick to lean cuts.

wherever possible, select dairy products with reduced or no fat. Avoiding utilising tropical oils that contain saturated fat.

• Try to use as little trans fat as feasible. In place of other fats, use canola oil for baking and olive oil for cooking.

• Cut back on your overall fat intake. Less than 10% of your total calories should come from fat, even if some fats are healthier than others and do have advantages. Decrease consumption of fried foods and high-fat baked items. Fruit can take the place of some or all of the fat in baked goods.

• Keep whole eggs away. When possible, replace egg substitutes for whole eggs.

• Limit your intake of other foods, notably organ meats and seafood, that are rich in cholesterol.

• Increase your intake of omega-3 fatty acids. Consume more seafood. For an additional boost in omega-3s, add nuts to salads and baked products.

• Increase your intake of whole grains. Consume baked products and bread made with whole grains. swap out white rice for brown. Prefer whole-grain pasta to normal spaghetti.

• Include more soluble fibre in your diet overall. Consume extra barley, beans, and oat bran.

Follow Jeffery F. Maurer where She shares Free recipes on Daily at Her online page and Also Reach Out to Her if You Have any questions:

Email: jefferyf.maurer@gmail.com

Instagram: Jeffery F. Maurer

Bonus

A. She Also Gives out Free Food and Shopping List Journals Which you can Print out and use.

B. Also get here Anti inflammatory diets cookbook, message Her via email for instant access.

To get this message Her with

Jeffery F. Maurer

"I Need Your Food and shopping list Journal" Via Email.

15 DAY MEAL PLAN

(Note: Use the Table of contents to Find the recipes)

WEEK 1

Breakfast: Vegan Ratatouille

Lunch: Summer Melon Salad

Dinner: Lemon Garlic Mackerel

Breakfast: Egg Foo Young

Lunch: Warm Soba and Tofu Salad

Dinner: Vietnamese Fish And Noodle Bowl

Breakfast: Creamed Rice

Lunch: Haddock Tacos with Spicy Slaw

Dinner: Chipotle Butternut Soup

Breakfast: Nutty Oat Cereal

Lunch: Shrimp and Pineapple Lettuce Wraps

Dinner: Fried Mahi-mahi

Breakfast: Cheesy Country Omelet

Lunch:

Dinner: Vegetable And Barley Soup

Breakfast: Italian Baked Omelet

Lunch:

Dinner: Grilled Scallops With Gremolata

Breakfast: Pumpkin Oatmeal Smoothies

Lunch:

Dinner: Indian Vegetable Soup

Week 2

Breakfast: Protein Cereal

Lunch: Meatball Linguine

Dinner: Chicken & Kale Soup

Breakfast: Maghrebi Poached Eggs

Lunch: Apple Cheesecake

Dinner: Chipotle Butternut Soup

Breakfast: Pumpkin Oatmeal Smoothie

Lunch: Spicy Catfish Tacos

Dinner: Italian Tomato Soup

Breakfast: Cranberry Orange Mixed Grain Granola

Lunch: Balsamic Rosemary Chicken

Dinner: Veggie Chicken Soup

Breakfast: Tofu Scramble With Tomato And Spinach

Lunch: Haddock Tacos With Spicy Slaw

Dinner: Chipotle Butternut Soup

Breakfast: Sweetato Bundt Cake

Lunch: Lemon Tarragon Turkey Medallions

Dinner: Cashew Butter Latte

Breakfast: Chocolate Chip Banana Muffins

Lunch: Sun-dried Tomato Chops

Dinner: Citrus Cod Bak

BASIC KITCHEN EQUIVALENTS AND CONVERSIONS

METRIC TO US COOKING cONVERSIONS

OVEN TEMPERATURES

250 F - 120°C

320 F - 160°C

350 F-180 C

400 F- 205 °C

425 F- 220 °C

LIQUID MEASUREMENTS CONVERSION CHART

1 CUP - 12 PINTS - 8 FLUID OUNCES - 1/4 QUART

2 CUPS - 1 PINT - 16 FLUID OUNCES - HALF QUART

32 FLUID OUNCES - 4 CUPS - 2 PINTS - A QUART - ¼ GALLON

1 GALLON - 16 CUPS - 8 PINTS - 4 QUARTS - 128 FLUID OUNCES

US TO METRIC COOKING CONVERSTONSION

1/5 TSP equals 1 ML

I TSP equals 5 ML

I TBSP equals 15 ML

IFL OUNCE equals 30 ML

I CUP equals 237 ML

I PINT (2 CUPS) equals 473 ML

1 QUART(4 CUPS) equals 95 LITER

1 GALLON (16 CUPS) equals 3.8 LITERS

1oz equals 28 GRAMS

I POUND equals 454 GRAMS

BUTTER

1 CUP BUTTER equals 2 STICKS equals 8 OUNCES equals 230 GRAMS equals 8 TABLESPOONS

WHAT DOES 1 CUP EQUAL

1 CUP equals 8 FLUID OUNCES

1 CUP equals 16 TABLESPOONS

1 CUP equals 48 TEASPOONS

1 CUP equals 1/2 PINT

1 CUP equals 1/4 QUART

1 CUP equals 1/16 GALLON

1 CUP equals 240 ML

BAKING PAN CONVERSIONS

9-INCH ROUND CAKE PAN equals 12 CUPS

10 INCH TUBE PAN equals 16 CUPS

11-INCH BUNDT PAN equals 12 CUPS

9-INCH SPRINGFORM PAN equals 10 CUPS

9X5 INCH LOAF PAN equals 8 CUPS

9-INCH SQUARE PAN equals 8 CUPS

BREAKFAST RECIPES

CREAMED RICE

Prep Time: 10 minutes

Time to Cook: 25 minutes

4 servings

INGREDIENTS:

1 cup of basmati rice

2 tablespoons of olive oil

1 finely chopped onion

2 minced garlic cloves.

Two glasses of low fat milk

2 tablespoons nutritional yeast

1 tablespoon cornflour

1 tsp. dried oregano

2 tablespoons of freshly chopped parsley

A pinch each of salt and pepper

INSTRUCTIONS:

1. Put the basmati rice in a medium pot and add cold water to cover it. Bring the pan to a boil over high heat, then reduce the heat and simmer for 12 minutes. Drain the rice in a sieve and rinse with cold water. Set aside.

2. In a big pot over medium heat, warm the oil. Add the onion and garlic and cook, stirring occasionally, for 5 minutes, until soft and fragrant.

3. Add the milk and boil the mixture gently. Corn flour and nutritional yeast should be whisked in gradually once the mixture has thickened.

4. Add the oregano, salt, pepper, and cooked basmati rice, and simmer for 5 minutes.

5. Add the parsley and then serve.

NUTRIENT CONTENT (PER SERVING):

Energy: 270 kcal

Fat: 8.5g

33.5g of carbohydrates

9.5g of protein

1.5g of fibre

0 g of cholesterol

HEALTH BENEFIT:

This creamed rice recipe is an excellent choice for those looking to reduce their cholesterol levels. The rice is low in cholesterol and the milk used is low-fat, helping to keep the overall cholesterol content of the dish down. Additionally, the olive oil provides healthy monounsaturated fats, and the nutritional yeast adds a boost of B-vitamins.

ROLLED OATS CEREAL

10 minutes for preparation

4 servings

INGREDIENTS:

200g or 2 cups of rolled oats

a ¼ cup (30g) of roughly chopped pecans

30g of walnuts, or 1/4 cup, roughly chopped

30g or 1/4 cup of sunflower seeds

30g or 1/4 cup of pumpkin seeds

1 teaspoon (5g) of cinnamon powder

1 gramme of ground nutmeg, or 1/4 teaspoon

olive oil, 2 tablespoons (30g)

A ¼ cup (60 grammes) of pure maple syrup

1/4 cup (60ml) of almond milk

INSTRUCTIONS:

1. Preheat oven to 175°C and line a baking sheet with parchment paper.

2. Combine rolled oats, pecans, walnuts, sunflower seeds, pumpkin seeds, cinnamon, and nutmeg in a large bowl.

3. Combine melted olive oil and maple syrup in another bowl.

4. Combine the wet and dry ingredients and stir until everything is thoroughly covered.

5. Spread the oat mixture onto the prepared baking sheet and bake for 12 minutes.

6. Take the food out of the oven and let it cool.

7. Store the oat cereal in an airtight container once it has cooled.

NUTRIENT CONTENT (PER SERVING):

140 calories

Fat: 6g

19g of carbohydrates

2g of fibre

5g protein

HEALTH BENEFIT:

Dietary fibre, which can help lower cholesterol and lower the risk of heart disease, is abundant in rolled oats. They are also a good source of complex carbs, plant-based protein, and a wide range of vitamins and minerals. The nuts and seeds in this cereal are a fantastic source of antioxidants, which aid in the prevention of chronic diseases.

INGREDIENT ALTERNATIVES:

You can use different nuts or seeds in their place if you don't have any of the specified nuts or seeds. You can also use honey or agave nectar in place of maple syrup. Every other cooking oil can be switched out for olive oil. Any other non-dairy milk can be switched out for almond milk.

EGG FOO YOUNG

15 minutes for preparation

2 servings

INGREDIENTS:

- 2 large eggs
- 3 tablespoons of plain flour
- 2 tablespoons of low-fat milk
- 2 tablespoons of vegetable oil
- 1/2 cup of chopped mushrooms
- 1/2 cup of sliced red peppers
- 1/2 cup of chopped onion
- 1/4 cup of cooked, diced ham
- 1/4 cup of cooked, diced chicken
- 2 tablespoons of reduced-sodium soy sauce
- 1/4 teaspoon of ground ginger
- 1/4 teaspoon of garlic powder

• Salt and pepper, to taste

• 1/4 cup of low-fat sour cream

INSTRUCTIONS:

1. In a medium bowl, mix the milk, eggs, and flour until combined.

2. In a big skillet over medium heat, warm the oil.

3. Include the mushrooms, red peppers, and onions and simmer for 5 minutes or until softened.

4. Add the chicken and gammon and simmer for an additional 3 minutes.

5. Add the soy sauce, ginger, garlic powder, salt, and pepper, and stir to combine.

6. Add the egg mixture to the vegetable mixture and cook for 5 minutes, or until the eggs are set.

7. Serve the egg foo young with the sour cream.

NUTRIENT CONTENT (PER SERVING):

238 calories

11g of carbohydrates

16g of protein

Fat: 13g

2g of fibre

HEALTH BENEFIT:

Egg foo young is a fantastic way to increase your daily intake of vegetables. The veggies include important vitamins, minerals, and antioxidants that support the health and proper operation of your body. This dish is ideal for anyone limiting their cholesterol consumption because the eggs are a rich source of protein and have low cholesterol. The addition of the ham and chicken provide an even greater source of protein, making this a complete meal.

INGREDIENT ALTERNATIVES:

You can use cooked prawn or tofu in place of the meat if you don't have any chicken or ham on hand. You may delete the beef and include more vegetables of your choice if you want a vegetarian version. Almond milk or any other non-dairy milk of your choosing can be used as a substitute if low-fat milk is not available. For a healthier alternative, you could also use Greek yogurt in place of the low-fat sour cream.

Jeffery F. Maurer

CRANBERRY HOTCAKES

20 minutes for preparation

6 servings.

INGREDIENTS:

• Two cups of plain flour (200g)

• Baking powder, 2 tablespoons (10g)

• Baking soda, 1 teaspoon (5g)

• ½ teaspoon salt (2g)

• Sugar, 2 tablespoons (25g)

• 2 eggs

• Two cups of skim milk (400ml)

• ¼ cup of vegetable oil (50ml)

• A half-cup of dried cranberries (50g)

Instructions

1. Combine the flour, baking powder, baking soda, salt, and sugar in a large bowl and stir to combine thoroughly.

2. Beat the eggs in another basin until they are frothy and light.

3. Add the milk and oil to the egg mixture and beat until combined.

4. Stir gently to mix, and gradually add the wet components to the dry ingredients.

5. Fold in the dried cranberries.

6. Heat a non-stick pan over medium heat.

7. When the pan is heated, spread the batter onto it in the correct proportions and cook the pancakes until bubbles appear on their tops.

8. Turn the hotcakes over and heat until both sides are golden brown.

9. Serve with butter, syrup, or your favorite topping.

NUTRIENT CONTENT (PER SERVING):

Energy: 187 kcal

Fat: 7.5 g

25 g of carbohydrates

5 g of protein

1 g of fibre

HEALTH BENEFIT:

The combination of vegetable oil and low-fat milk in this recipe helps to lower the cholesterol content of the hotcakes, making them a healthier alternative to traditional hotcakes. This is a wholesome and delectable breakfast option since cranberries offer an extra burst of vitamins and antioxidants.

INGREDIENT ALTERNATIVES:

If you'd like to make this recipe even healthier, you can substitute the vegetable oil for applesauce or mashed banana. You can also replace the low-fat milk with almond or soy milk. For a vegan version, you can use flax eggs instead of regular eggs.

AVO BRUSCHETTA

6 servings

20 minutes for preparation

Time to Cook: 10 minutes

INGREDIENTS:

2 pitted and peeled ripe avocados

2 smashed garlic cloves

2 teaspoons of lemon juice that has just been squeezed

12 slices of whole wheat baguette

1 small red onion, diced

2 tablespoons extra-virgin olive oil

1 tablespoon freshly chopped parsley

salt and pepper to taste

INSTRUCTIONS:

1. Set oven temperature to 180°C.

2. Arrange the pieces of baguette on a baking sheet.

3. Bake for 10 minutes, or until the sides are just starting to turn golden.

4. Meanwhile, prepare the Avo Bruschetta topping.

5. Use a fork or potato masher to mash the avocados in a medium bowl.

6. Add the parsley, garlic, onion, lemon juice, olive oil, salt, and pepper.

7. Mix all the ingredients together until combined.

8. Once the baguette slices are ready, top each one with a spoonful of the Avo Bruschetta mixture

9. Serve right away.

NUTRIENT CONTENT (PER SERVING):

160 calories

20 g of carbohydrates

4 g of protein

0 mg of cholesterol

4 g of fibre

HEALTH BENEFIT:

Avocado Bruschetta is a fantastic option for anyone on a low-cholesterol diet. Whole wheat baguette offers complex carbohydrates and fibre, while avocados offer good fats that may decrease cholesterol levels. This mixture of ingredients creates a delightful and nutritious snack that you can eat guilt-free.

INGREDIENT ALTERNATIVES:

You can also use fresh herbs in place of parsley, like cilantro or basil. Finally, you can omit the garlic from the recipe if you don't like it.

VEGETARIAN SCRAMBLE

Prep Time: 10 minutes

Servings: 2

INGREDIENTS:

- 2 tablespoons of olive oil
- 2 cloves garlic, minced
- 2 medium onions, chopped
- 2 large carrots, diced
- 2 large mushrooms, diced
- 2 cups cooked quinoa
- 1/2 teaspoon ground turmeric
- 1/2 teaspoon ground cumin
- 1/4 teaspoon ground coriander
- 1/4 teaspoon red pepper flakes
- 1/2 teaspoon sea salt
- 2 tablespoons nutritional yeast

- 1/2 cup chopped fresh parsley
- 2 tablespoons chopped fresh dill
- 2 tablespoons chopped fresh chives

INSTRUCTIONS:

1. In a big skillet over medium heat, warm the olive oil.

2. Add the garlic, onions, and carrots and cook, stirring occasionally, for 5 minutes or until the vegetables are just softened.

3. Add the mushrooms and simmer for 3 minutes, stirring periodically, or until they are just beginning to soften.

4. Add the cooked quinoa and whisk in the salt, red pepper flakes, cumin, turmeric, and coriander.

5. Simmer for 3 minutes, stirring regularly, or until the spices are fragrant.

6. Add the nutritional yeast, parsley, dill, and chives and stir to combine.

7. Simmer for 2 minutes, stirring periodically, or until the herbs have wilted.

8. Present heat.

NUTRIENT CONTENT (PER SERVING):

216 calories

Fat: 8.1g

27.2g of carbohydrates

7.2g of protein

Salt: 832 mg

HEALTH BENEFIT:

The minimal cholesterol in this vegetarian scramble has a variety of health advantages. In order to lower cholesterol levels, quinoa, veggies, and herbs are wonderful sources of fibre, vitamins, and minerals. The spices and olive oil have anti-inflammatory properties and lower blood pressure. Without the additional cholesterol of cheese, nutritional yeast gives a cheesy flavour.

INGREDIENT ALTERNATIVES:

Cooked brown rice or other whole grains can be used as a substitute for quinoa if you don't have any. Other veggies like bell peppers, spinach, or zucchini can be used as a substitute. If you don't have any of the herbs, you can omit them or substitute dried herbs. Other spices that you can use instead include curry powder, garam masala, and smoked paprika. You can remove it or use grated Parmesan cheese in its place if you don't have nutritional yeast on hand.

ITALIAN BAKED OMELET

20 minutes for preparation

4 servings

INGREDIENTS:

6 eggs

1/3 cup of low fat milk

2 tablespoons of extra virgin olive oil

1/2 cup grated Parmesan cheese

1/3 cup finely chopped red pepper, mushrooms, and zucchini

1/4 teaspoon dried oregano,

1/4 teaspoon salt

1/4 teaspoon freshly ground black pepper.

INSTRUCTIONS:

1. Set the oven to 175 degrees C.

2. Grease a baking dish that is 8 inches square.

3. Combine the milk and eggs in a medium bowl.

4. In a big skillet over medium heat, warm the oil. Add the onion, red pepper, mushrooms, and zucchini, and simmer for 5 minutes or until the vegetables are tender.

5. Add salt, pepper, and oregano.

6. Pour the egg mixture into the baking dish.

7. Top with the vegetable mixture and sprinkle with the Parmesan cheese.

8. Bake for about 25 minutes in the preheated oven, or until the eggs are set.

NUTRIENT CONTENT (PER SERVING):

176 calories

Fat total: 10.2g

3.4g of saturated fat

5.4g of carbohydrates

14.6g of protein

HEALTH BENEFIT:

the Italian Baked Omelet is a fantastic dish. The eggs used in this dish provide a great source of protein and are also high in essential vitamins and minerals. The vegetables provide essential vitamins, minerals, and dietary fiber, while the cheese and olive oil provide healthy fats. This dish is also a good source of iron, calcium, and Vitamin A.

INGREDIENT ALTERNATIVES:

If you would like to reduce the fat and cholesterol in this dish, you can substitute the eggs for egg whites or egg substitutes. You can also substitute the olive oil for a heart-healthy oil such as canola oil. If desired, you can also substitute the Parmesan cheese for a low-fat or non-dairy cheese.

NUTTY OAT CEREAL

10 minutes for preparation

4 servings

INGREDIENTS:

Two cups of big-flakes oats (200g)

Chopped 1/4 cup of toasted almonds (30g)

1/4 cup chopped toasted hazelnuts (30g)

1/4 cup chopped roasted walnuts (30g)

¼ cup of sunflower seeds (30g)

Sesame seeds, 2 tablespoons (20g)

Flaxseeds, 2 teaspoons (20g)

pumpkin seeds, 2 tablespoons (20g)

honey, 1/4 cup (60ml)

olive oil, 2 tablespoons (30ml)

cinnamon, 2 tablespoons (14g)

nutmeg, 1 teaspoon (2g)

INSTRUCTIONS:

1. Turn on the oven to 180 °C.

2. Spread the flaxseeds, pumpkin seeds, sunflower seeds, sesame seeds, almonds, hazelnuts, and walnuts on a baking sheet.

3. Drizzle the honey and olive oil over the oats and nuts, and sprinkle the cinnamon and nutmeg over the top.

4. Bake the oats and nuts in the preheated oven for 8 to 10 minutes, stirring halfway through, or until they are fragrant and gently golden.

5. Take out of the oven, then allow to cool.

6. You can Keep for up to two weeks in an airtight jar.

NUTRIENT CONTENT (PER SERVING):

Energy: 247 kcal

7.3g of protein

Fat: 17.2g

20.5g of carbohydrates

3.2g of fibre

HEALTH BENEFIT:

The oats are a great source of dietary fiber, which helps to reduce cholesterol levels in the body. The nuts and seeds are packed with healthy fats and essential vitamins and minerals that help to support overall health. The olive oil is a healthy saturated fat that can help to raise good cholesterol levels while reducing bad cholesterol. The honey and spices add a touch of sweetness and flavor, making this a tasty and nutritious breakfast cereal.

INGREDIENT ALTERNATIVES:

- Maple syrup or agave nectar can be substituted for honey if you don't have any on hand.
- You can substitute melted butter or vegetable oil for olive oil if you don't have any on hand.
- You can use any other nut, such as cashews, macadamias, or pecans if you don't have almonds.
- You can use any other nut, such as almonds, walnuts, or macadamias if you don't have hazelnuts.

- Almonds, hazelnuts, or macadamia nuts can be substituted for walnuts if you don't have any on hand.

PROTEIN CEREAL

Prep Time: 10 minutes

Servings: 6

INGREDIENTS:

2 tablespoons chia seeds

1/4 teaspoon ground cinnamon

1/4 teaspoon sea salt

2 tablespoons almond butter

2 tablespoons honey

2 tablespoons chopped almonds

2 cups rolled oats

1 cup vanilla soy milk

1/4 cup raisins

2 teaspoons chia seeds

INSTRUCTIONS:

1. Set oven temperature to (175 degrees Celsius).

2. Combine the rolled oats, soy milk, banana puree, raisins, chia seeds, cinnamon, and sea salt a big bowl. Mix everything together until it's all spread equally.

3. Spoon the oat mixture into a baking dish that is 23cm.

4. Spread the oat mixture with almond butter.

5. Pour honey on top of the almond butter.

6. Sprinkle chopped almonds over the top of the oat mixture.

7. Bake for 25 minutes in the preheated oven.

8. Let the food cool before serving.

NUTRIENT CONTENT (PER SERVING):

236 calories.

Fat 10.5 grammes

30.4 grammes of carbohydrates overall

Fiber: 4.2 grammes

8.4 grammes of protein

HEALTH BENEFIT:

Oats are a great source of protein and dietary fibre, making them a wise choice for people trying to lower their cholesterol. Chia seeds are added for even more fibre and protein, and almonds offer wholesome fats and more protein. The raisins also contribute a small amount of natural sweetness, in addition to the honey, banana, and honey. For a filling and delicious meal to start the day, try this protein cereal.

INGREDIENT ALTERNATIVES:

There are many substitutes you can use if you don't have or don't like one of the components in this recipe. You can use bulgur wheat, rolled quinoa, or even crushed cornflakes in place of the oats. Almond milk, oat milk, or any other dairy-free substitute can be used in place of soy milk. You can substitute walnuts, pecans, or cashews for the almonds. You can substitute maple syrup or agave nectar for the honey.

Finally, hemp or flax seeds may be substituted for chia seeds.

Jeffery F. Maurer

MAGHREBI POACHED EGGS

10 minutes for preparation

4 servings

INGREDIENTS:

4 large free-range eggs

- 2 tablespoons of olive oil

- 1 onion, chopped

- 2 cloves garlic, chopped

- 2 teaspoons ground coriander

- 2 teaspoons ground cumin

- 2 teaspoons ground paprika

- 1 teaspoon of salt

- 1 teaspoon freshly ground black pepper

- 2 tablespoons tomato paste

- 2 cups of vegetable stock

- 2 tablespoons of chopped fresh parsley

- 2 tablespoons of chopped fresh mint

INGREDIENTS:

1. In a big pot set over medium heat, warm the olive oil.

2. Stir in the onion, garlic, coriander, cumin, paprika, salt, and pepper, and cook for an additional 5 minutes, or until the onion is tender.

3. Add the tomato paste and blend by stirring.

4. Add the vegetable stock and bring the mixture to a boil.

5. Lower the temperature to a low simmer for 5 minutes.

6. Crack the eggs into the saucepan one at a time, making sure they are evenly spaced.

5. Continue to simmer.

8. Switch off the heat and give the eggs five minutes to rest in the sauce.

9. Using a slotted spoon, remove the eggs and set them on a platter.

10. Add fresh mint and parsley as a garnish.

11. Serve and enjoy

NUTRIENT CONTENT (PER SERVING):

204 calories

11.3g of protein

9.5g of carbohydrates

2.6g of fibre

212 mg of cholesterol

HEALTH BENEFIT:

This recipe for Maghrebi Poached Eggs is a wonderful way to have a delectable Breakfast while simultaneously managing your cholesterol levels. The vegetables in the recipe offer fibre and other necessary minerals, and olive oil is a heart-healthy fat. Without the added cholesterol found in red meat or processed meats, eggs themselves are a healthy source of protein.

INGREDIENT ALTERNATIVES:

you might use coconut or avocado oil for the olive oil in the recipe. In addition, you can substitute any sort of stock, including chicken or beef stock, for vegetable stock. Moreover, if preferred, you can substitute dried herbs for fresh mint and parsley.

Jeffery F. Maurer

CHEESY COUNTRY OMELET

10 minutes for preparation

4 servings

INGREDIENTS:

1 teaspoon olive oil

4 large eggs

4 tablespoons skim milk

2 teaspoons finely chopped bell pepper

1 cup diced cooked ham

½ cup shredded reduced-fat cheese

To taste, salt and pepper

Instructions:

1. Beat the eggs, milk, salt, and pepper together in a medium bowl until well blended.

2. In a big nonstick skillet, heat the olive oil over medium heat.

3. Add the onion and bell pepper and sauté for 3 minutes or until tender.

4. Add the egg mixture to the skillet and simmer for 2 minutes or until nearly set.

5. Add the gammon and cheese, and heat for 2 minutes or until the eggs are fully cooked.

6. Present the warm omelet.

NUTRIENT CONTENT (PER SERVING):

Energy: 152 kcal

Protein: 13.7 g

Carbohydrates: 2.7 g

Fat: 8.4 g

158 mg of cholesterol

Salt: 483 mg

0.3 g of fibre

HEALTH BENEFIT:

Due to its low cholesterol and saturated fat content, this Cheesy Country Omelet is a fantastic choice for a low-cholesterol diet. Vegetables are a rich source of vitamins and minerals, while eggs are a fantastic supply of protein. The monounsaturated fats found in olive oil, which have been shown to decrease cholesterol levels, are another excellent source of nutrition.

INGREDIENT ALTERNATIVES:

If you don't have any onions or bell peppers, you can use other veggies instead, like spinach, mushrooms, or zucchini. Other lean protein sources, including chicken or turkey, can be used in place of the ham. If low-fat cheese is not available, you can substitute low-fat or full-fat cheese; however, the nutritional facts will vary as a result.

TOFU SCRAMBLE WITH TOMATO AND SPINACH

10 minutes for preparation

4 servings

INGREDIENTS:

- 340g extra firm tofu, drained and crumbled
- 1 clove garlic, minced
- 1 teaspoon olive oil
- 1/2 teaspoon turmeric
- 1/2 teaspoon ground cumin
- 1/4 teaspoon ground coriander
- 1/4 teaspoon paprika
- 1/4 teaspoon sea salt
- 1/4 teaspoon freshly ground black pepper
- 2 tomatoes, diced
- 2 cups baby spinach leaves, chopped

- 2 tablespoons nutritional yeast

Instructions

1. Combine the crumbled tofu, garlic, olive oil, turmeric, cumin, coriander, paprika, salt, and pepper in a medium bowl and stir to blend.

2. Heat a large skillet over medium heat. Add the tofu mixture to the pan and cook, stirring occasionally, for 8 minutes, or until the tofu is lightly browned.

3. Add the tomatoes and spinach to the pan and heat for 2 minutes, or until the spinach wilts and the tomatoes soften.

4. Switch off the hob and add the nutritional yeast.

5. Serve and enjoy

Nutritional Details

NUTRIENT CONTENT (PER SERVING):

119 calories

9.8g of protein

8.9g of carbohydrates

0 mg of cholesterol

Salt: 333 mg

2.7g of fibre

HEALTH BENEFIT:

This quick and simple dish is a fantastic way to get fibre and plant-based protein. This dish's tofu is a fantastic source of protein, and the tomatoes and spinach also offer a healthy serving of fibre. While tofu is a fantastic source of plant-based protein and is naturally low in cholesterol.

INGREDIENT ALTERNATIVES:

Grated Parmesan cheese can be used as a substitute if you don't have nutritional yeast. You may also add some finely chopped jalapenos or red pepper flakes to the recipe if you want to make it hotter. In addition, you can use different veggies in place of tomatoes and spinach, like bell peppers, mushrooms, or zucchini.

CRANBERRY ORANGE MIXED GRAIN GRANOLA

15 minutes for preparation

10 servings

INGREDIENTS:

• 2 cups rolled oats

• ¾ cup sunflower seeds

• ¾ cup pumpkin seeds

• ¼ cup sesame seeds

ingredients:

• ½ cup wheat germ

• ½ cup oat bran

• ½ cup unsweetened coconut flakes

• ¼ teaspoon salt

• ¼ cup honey

• ¼ cup vegetable oil

• 1 teaspoon vanilla extract

- ½ teaspoon ground cinnamon
- 1 cup dried cranberries
- ½ cup chopped dried orange peel

INSTRUCTIONS:

1. Set oven temperature to 350°F (175°C).

2. Combine the rolled oats, wheat germ, oat bran, coconut flakes, sesame seeds, sunflower seeds, pumpkin seeds, and salt in a large bowl.

3. Combine the honey, vegetable oil, vanilla essence, and ground cinnamon in another bowl.

4. Pour honey mixture over oat mixture and stir until everything is evenly coated.

5. Spread granola mixture onto a parchment-lined baking sheet and bake for 15 minutes, stirring once halfway through.

6. Remove from the oven, then allow to cool.

7. After it has cooled, mix in the chopped dry orange peel and dried cranberries.

8. Serve and enjoy!!

9. You can Keep for up to two weeks in an airtight jar.

NUTRIENT CONTENT (PER SERVING):

- 268 calories
- 13g of total fat
- 0 mg of cholesterol.
- 61 mg of sodium
- 32g of total carbohydrates

• 4g of dietary fibre

• 6g of protein

HEALTH BENEFIT:

This recipe for low-cholesterol food is a fantastic method to increase the amount of protein and fibre in your diet without increasing the amount of saturated fat or cholesterol. While the wheat germ and oat bran provide an additional boost of protein, the oats and seeds are a fantastic source of dietary fibre. The natural sweetness is provided by honey, vegetable oil, and dried fruit, while a bit of spice is added by the cinnamon. All of these components combine to create a tasty and wholesome granola that is ideal for a low-cholesterol diet.

INGREDIENT ALTERNATIVES:

• You can use an equal amount of flaxseed meal if you don't have wheat germ.

• You can use an equal amount of wheat bran if you don't have any oat bran.

• Dried cherries or raisins can be used in place of dried cranberries

• You can use an equal amount of dried apricots or apples in place of the chopped dried orange peel if you don't have any on hand.

BLUEBERRY ALMOND BREAKFAST BOWL

10 minutes to prepare

1 serving

INGREDIENTS

• 50g (12 cup) of rolled oats

• Two teaspoons (25g) of almond slivers

• Ground flaxseed, 2 teaspoons (15 g)

• 1 tsp. (5 g) of honey

• 150g of fresh blueberries in 1 cup

• almond milk, 125 ml (1/2 cup)

INSTRUCTIONS

1. Combine the ground flaxseed, slivered almonds, and rolled oats in a bowl.

2. Combine the blueberries, honey, and other ingredients.

3. Pour the almond milk over the mixture and swirl to incorporate.

4. Let the mixture rest for five minutes, or until the oats are soft.

5. Serve in a bowl and enjoy.

NUTRIENT CONTENT (PER SERVING):

Energy: 298 kcal

40 g of carbohydrates

11 g of protein

11 g of fat

8 g of fibre

11 g of sugar

HEALTH BENEFIT:

A low-cholesterol, healthful breakfast like this blueberry almond bowl is a terrific way to start the day. Fibre from oats is a fantastic source of enhancing digestive health. A good supply of monounsaturated fats, which can lower harmful cholesterol levels and enhance heart health, is found in almonds. Omega-3 fatty acids, which might lessen inflammation and enhance heart health, are abundant in ground flaxseed. Antioxidants from blueberries are a fantastic source for lowering inflammation and enhancing general health. Calcium from almond milk is a wonderful source that can help lower cholesterol and strengthen bones.

INGREDIENT ALTERNATIVES:

• Other varieties of oats, such as steel-cut or quick-cooking oats, are also acceptable.

• You can substitute different nuts, like cashews or walnuts.

• You can substitute chia or pumpkin seeds for the others.

• Honey can be exchanged for agave nectar or maple syrup.

• You can substitute different berries, like blackberries or raspberries.

• You can substitute soy or oat milk for regular milk.

PUMPKIN OATMEAL SMOOTHIE

5 minutes for preparation

1 serving

INGREDIENTS:

- ½ cup (120ml) of unsweetened almond milk
- ½ cup (120ml) of pumpkin puree
- ¼ cup (30g) of old-fashioned rolled oats
- 1 banana, peeled and sliced
- 2 tablespoons (30ml) of maple syrup
- ½ teaspoon (2.5ml) of ground cinnamon
- ¼ teaspoon (1.25ml) of ground nutmeg
- ⅛ teaspoon (0.625ml) of ground ginger
- A handful of ice cubes

INSTRUCTIONS:

1. In a blender, combine the almond milk, banana, oats, pumpkin puree, maple syrup, cinnamon, nutmeg, and ginger. Blend until smooth.

2.. After adding the ice, blend the smoothie once more until it is thick and creamy.

3. Transfer the smoothie to a glass, then sip it.

NUTRIENT CONTENT (PER SERVING):

• 268 kcal of calories

• 3g of total fat

• 0g of saturated fat

 0mg of cholesterol.

• Salt: 115 mg

54g of total carbohydrates

•5g of dietary fiber

• 21g of total sugars

• 5g of protein

HEALTH BENEFIT:

This smoothie is a wonderful way to start your morning with a burst of nourishment. The pumpkin puree gives the smoothie a creamy texture and is rich in fibre, vitamins, and minerals. The banana adds a touch of natural sweetness and creaminess while the oats offer an excellent dose of fibre and protein. A delightful autumnal flavour is added to the smoothie through the mixture of spices.

INGREDIENTS:

• You can substitute any other sort of milk or nut milk substitute if you don't have almond milk.

• You can substitute butternut squash or sweet potato puree for pumpkin puree if you don't have any.

• Honey or agave nectar can be substituted for maple syrup in this recipe.

• You can use pumpkin pie spice if you don't have ground cinnamon, nutmeg, and ginger.

• You can eliminate the ice cubes or substitute frozen fruit if you don't have any on hand.

SALAD
RECIPE

Salads

SMOKED GOUDA AND TOMATO SANDWICH

Prep Time: 10 minutes

4 servings

INGREDIENTS:

four slices of whole wheat bread

four ounces of thinly sliced smoked gouda cheese

two ripe tomatoes

two tablespoons of mayonnaise

two tablespoons of chopped fresh basil

salt and pepper to taste.

INSTRUCTIONS:

1. Set a sizable skillet over medium heat to preheat.

2. Spread the mayonnaise over one side of each piece of bread.

3. Place two slices of bread, mayonnaise side down, into the preheated skillet.

4. Arrange the tomato slices and cheese slices on top of one of the bread slices in the skillet.

5. Sprinkle the chopped basil over the tomatoes.

6. Top with the remaining slice of bread, mayonnaise side up.

7. Heat for about 3 minutes on each side, or until the cheese is melted and the bread is golden brown.

8. Take the dish off the fire and add salt and pepper to taste.

9. To serve, split the sandwich in half.

NUTRIENT CONTENT (PER SERVING):

347 calories

17 g total fat

8 g of saturated fat

30-mg cholesterol

NaCl: 564 mg

34 g of carbohydrates

5 g of fibre

16 g of protein

HEALTH BENEFIT:

The tomatoes are a fantastic source of vitamins and minerals, and the whole wheat bread offers a wonderful quantity of fibre. This sandwich will help you feel full and pleased because it is a great source of protein.

INGREDIENT ALTERNATIVES:

You can use cheddar or provolone cheese in place of smoked Gouda if you don't have any of that sort of cheese on hand. Also, you can use any bread variety you prefer, including rye, sourdough, and white bread. You can use hummus or plain Greek yoghurt for mayonnaise if you don't have any. Last but not least, you can use dried basil or other herbs like oregano or thyme if you don't have access to fresh basil.

MIXED BERRY CHICKEN SALAD

Prep Time: 15 minutes

4 servings

Ingredients:
- 250g boneless chicken breasts, diced
- 200g mixed berries – raspberries, blueberries, blackberries and cranberries
- 100g red grapes, halved
- 2 large celery stalks, diced
- 1/4 teaspoon garlic powder
- 1/4 teaspoon onion powder
- 2 tablespoons olive oil
- 2 tablespoons lemon juice
- 2 tablespoons white wine vinegar

- 1/4 teaspoon sea salt
- 1/4 teaspoon ground black pepper
- 2 tablespoons chopped fresh mint
- 2 tablespoons chopped fresh parsley
- 2 tablespoons chopped fresh basil

Instructions:

1. In a big skillet over medium-high heat, warm the olive oil.

2. Add the diced chicken and season with black pepper, sea salt, garlic powder, and onion powder. Sauté for about 10 minutes, or until the chicken is thoroughly done.

3. Add the mixed berries, red grapes, celery, lemon juice, white wine vinegar, fresh mint, parsley, and basil to the big bowl with the cooked chicken.

4. Gently blend by stirring.

5. Serve the salad at room temperature, or chilled.

NUTRIENT CONTENT (PER SERVING):

Energy: 216 kcal

9.7 g of carbohydrates

19.7 g of protein; 10.6 g of fat

1.7 g of saturated fat

57 mg of cholesterol

Salt: 263 mg

2.6 g of fibre

HEALTH BENEFIT:

This salad is a great alternative for a supper. It is loaded with protein and fibre from the chicken, celery, and berries, as well as beneficial fats from the olive oil. Moreover, it contains omega-3 fatty acids from berries and heart-healthy polyunsaturated fats from olive oil. While the lemon juice and white wine vinegar give the salad a sharp flavor, the fresh herbs contribute flavour and antioxidants.

INGREDIENT ALTERNATIVES:

You can make a few modifications if you don't have access to all of the Ingredients. In place of the chicken, you can use turkey, tofu, or tempeh. You can use other berries of your choice in place of mixed berries, such as strawberries, blueberries, or blackberries. The celery can be swapped out for diced bell peppers, and the red grapes can be replaced with seedless green grapes. Dried herbs can be used in place of fresh ones, and olive oil or avocado oil can be used in place of olive oil.

WARM SOBA AND TOFU SALAD

15 minutes for preparation

2 servings

Ingredients:

140g soba noodles

1 tablespoon sesame oil

2 minced garlic cloves

200g diced firm tofu

2 grated carrots

2 thinly sliced spring onions.

2 teaspoons sesame seeds

2-tablespoons of tamari (or soy sauce)

1 tsp honey

2 tbsp rice vinegar

2 tablespoons neutral oil (such as sunflower or vegetable oil)

INSTRUCTIONS:

1. Bring a lot of water to a rolling boil in a large pot. Add the soba noodles and cook for 6-7 minutes, or until al dente. Drain and rinse with cold water to stop the cooking process.

2. In a large skillet over medium heat, warm the sesame oil. Cook the tofu for 3–4 minutes, stirring occasionally, after adding the garlic.

3. Stir in the carrots, spring onions, and sesame seeds, and simmer for an additional 2 to 3 minutes.

4. Combine the tamari, rice vinegar, honey, and neutral oil in a small bowl.

5. Place the cooked noodles in the skillet and top with the salad dressing. Mix the noodles

and vegetables with the dressing until it is distributed evenly.

6. Serve warm or at room temperature.

NUTRIENT CONTENT (PER SERVING):

395 calories

42.3g of carbohydrates

11.5g of protein

Fat: 18.8g

594 mg of sodium

5.2g of fibre

HEALTH BENEFIT:

Being low in saturated fat and high in fibre, this Warm Soba and Tofu Salad is a fantastic option for a low-cholesterol diet. Buckwheat, a whole grain that is high in fibre, vitamins, and minerals, is used to make the soba noodles. Tofu offers a variety of necessary amino acids and is a fantastic source of plant-based protein. Sesame seeds, carrots, and spring onions give flavour and additional nutrients.

INGREDIENT ALTERNATIVES:

You can use rice noodles, udon, ramen, or other varieties of noodles in place of soba noodles if you don't have any on hand. You may swap out the honey for a plant-based sweetener like agave syrup or maple syrup to make the recipe vegan. You can substitute olive oil or avocado oil for sesame oil if you don't have any on hand. Last but not least, you can use coconut aminos in place of tamari or soy sauce if you don't have either.

TUNISIAN SPICED CARROTS

10 minutes for preparation

20 minutes for cooking

4 servings

INGREDIENTS:

4 huge carrots, peeled and sliced into 1-inch slices,

2 tablespoons of olive oil

1 teaspoon each of cumin and paprika

1 teaspoon of coriander, ground

1/2 tsp. cinnamon

¼ teaspoon each of ground ginger and turmeric

Salt and pepper to taste

INSTRUCTIONS:

1 Start by setting the oven to 375°F (190°C).

2. Place carrots on a baking sheet and drizzle with olive oil.

3. Combine salt, pepper, cumin, paprika, coriander, cinnamon, ginger, turmeric, and it in a small bowl.

4. Sprinkle the carrots with the spice mixture and toss to incorporate.

5. Bake the carrots for 20 minutes, or until they are soft.

6. Present hot.

NUTRIENT CONTENT (PER SERVING):

Energy: 87 kcal

Fat: 5 g

10 g of carbohydrates

3 g of fibre

1 g of protein

Salt: 183 mg

HEALTH BENEFIT:

Tunisian spiced carrots are a simple, delectable way to increase the number of vegetables in your meals. They are rich in fibre, vitamin A, vitamin C, potassium, and other vitamins and minerals. The spices used in this recipe are both anti-inflammatory and high in antioxidants. These carrots are a fantastic source of good fats, which are crucial for controlling cholesterol levels.

INGREDIENT ALTERNATIVES:

You can use any other spices you have on hand as a substitute if you don't have all of the ones stated in the recipe. , instead of cumin, paprika, coriander, cinnamon, ginger, and turmeric, you may substitute a blend of garlic powder, oregano, and chilli powder. Other oils, including olive oil or avocado oil, can be used in place of olive oil.

LIME BRUSSELS SPROUTS

Prep Time: 10 minutes

4 servings

INGREDIENTS:

450g trimmed Brussels sprouts

2 tablespoons olive oil

2 tablespoons lime juice

1 minced garlic clove

sea salt and freshly crushed black pepper to taste

2 tablespoons coriander, finely chopped.

INSTRUCTIONS:

1. Set the oven to 400°F (200°C).

2. Place Brussels sprouts in a single layer on a baking sheet.

3. Combine olive oil, lime juice, and garlic in a small bowl.

4. Sprinkle the Brussels sprouts with the mixture. Add salt and pepper to taste.

5. Roast for 15 minutes, or until tender, in a preheated oven.

6. Take out of the oven, then top with freshly chopped coriander.

7. Present hot.

NUTRIENT CONTENT (PER SERVING):

• Calories: 92 kcal

• Protein: 3.7g

• Fat: 6.8g

• Carbohydrates: 6.1g

• Fiber: 3.2g

- Sodium: 12mg
- Cholesterol: 0mg

HEALTH BENEFIT:

Vitamin C, folate, and potassium are just a few of the vitamins and minerals that are abundant in Brussels sprouts. They are also a fantastic source of dietary fibre, which supports regularity and healthy digestion. In addition to giving the food flavour, the inclusion of lime juice and garlic has additional health advantages. Lime juice is a fantastic source of vitamin C, and garlic is a natural antibiotic.

INGREDIENT ALTERNATIVES:

This recipe can be easily modified to utilize other vegetables, such as cauliflower, broccoli, and carrots if you don't like Brussels sprouts. Other healthy cooking oils, including olive oil or avocado oil, can be used in place of olive oil. You can use lemon or balsamic vinegar in place of the lime juice if you want a low-carb option. Finally, you can use vegan butter for the olive oil if you're looking for a vegan version.

SKILLET-ROASTED SWEET POTATOES

10 minutes for preparation

4 servings

INGREDIENTS:

Four medium sweet potatoes, peeled and chopped into 2 cm cubes,

2 tablespoons of olive oil

2 teaspoons each of sea salt, freshly ground black pepper, ground cumin, and dried oregano

2 minced garlic cloves

INSTRUCTIONS:

1. Set the oven to 200 degrees Celsius (400 F).

2. Toss the garlic, cumin, oregano, salt, and olive oil with the sweet potatoes in a big bowl. Combine by tossing.

3. Arrange the sweet potatoes on a sizable baking sheet and bake for 20 to 25 minutes, or until they are soft and just beginning to turn golden brown.

4. Present hot.

NUTRIENT CONTENT (PER SERVING):

Calories: 147

- Total Fat: 7.6 g

- Saturated Fat: 1.1 g

- Cholesterol: 0 mg

- Sodium: 416 mg

- Total Carbohydrates: 19.3 g

- Dietary Fiber: 3.2 g

- Sugars: 3.6 g

- Protein: 2.3 g

HEALTH BENEFIT:

Sweet potatoes are a great source of dietary fibre, vitamins, minerals, and antioxidants, which are all beneficial to your health. In addition to lowering LDL (bad) cholesterol, fibre also supports general health by supplying vitamins, minerals, and antioxidants. Olive oil, spices, and garlic are combined to give the dish flavour and nutrition.

INGREDIENT ALTERNATIVES:

-Sweet potatoes can be swapped out for other root vegetables like yams, carrots, or beets in a recipe.

- Healthy oils like avocado oil and olive oil can be used in place of olive oil.

- Himalayan or Celtic sea salt can be used in place of regular table salt.

- Other spices, such as smoked paprika, chilli powder, or turmeric, can be used in place of ground cumin.

- Fresh oregano, thyme, or rosemary can be used in place of dried oregano.

- Shallots and onions can be used in place of garlic.

PIQUANT NAVY BEANS

45 minutes for preparation

4 servings

INGREDIENTS:

- 2 cups navy beans
- 2 tablespoons olive oil
- 2 tablespoons tomato paste
- 2 cloves garlic, minced
- 1 red onion, finely chopped
- 1 teaspoon dried oregano
- 1 teaspoon ground cumin
- ½ teaspoon smoked paprika
- 2 tablespoons red wine vinegar
- 2 tablespoons honey
- 2 tablespoons fresh parsley, chopped
- Salt and pepper to taste

INSTRUCTIONS:

1. Let the navy beans soak all night in cold water.

2. After the beans have been rinsed and drained, put them in a big saucepan and fill it with fresh water. Bring to a boil, then reduce the heat and simmer for 30 minutes or until the beans are tender. Drain and set aside.

3. In a big skillet over medium heat, warm the olive oil. Add the garlic and onion and sauté for 5 minutes or until the onion is translucent.

4. Add the paprika, cumin, oregano, and tomato paste and stir to blend.

5. Add the cooked navy beans and mix to combine.

6. Add the honey, parsley, and red wine vinegar and whisk to incorporate. You can also use fresh herbs in place of dried ones.

7. Continue to cook the beans for a further 5 to 10 minutes while stirring periodically.

8. Serve and enjoy!!

NUTRIENT CONTENT (PER SERVING):

210 calories

Fat: 4.2g

37.1g of carbohydrates

8.8g of protein

5.3g of fibre

HEALTH BENEFIT:

Navy beans are a fantastic source of fibre and protein, both of which can decrease cholesterol. Healthy fats from red wine vinegar and olive oil can help lower the risk of heart disease. Antioxidants from tomato paste and spices can aid in reducing inflammation. Navy beans are also a great source of vitamins and minerals like potassium, magnesium, and iron.

INGREDIENT ALTERNATIVES:

• Instead of navy beans, you can use white beans or black beans.

• In place of the honey, you can use water or vegetable broth if you're vegan.

• Red pepper flakes or cayenne pepper can be added to the meal to increase its heat.

• Fresh herbs like rosemary or thyme can be added to a dish to enhance its flavour.

ROCKET & GOAT CHEESE SALAD

10 minutes for preparation

4 servings

INGREDIENTS:

¼ cup of toasted pine nuts

2 large bunches of rocket

200g goat cheese

4 tablespoons extra virgin olive oil

2 tablespoons balsamic vinegar

1 squeezed garlic clove

salt, and freshly ground black pepper.

INSTRUCTIONS:

1. Place the rocket in a big dish after washing and drying it.

2. Add the goat cheese in crumbles to the basin.

3. Combine the olive oil, balsamic vinegar, garlic, salt, and pepper in a small bowl.

4. Drizzle the cheese and rocket with the dressing. Combine by tossing.

5. Finish by adding toasted pine nuts, then serve.

NUTRIENT CONTENT (PER SERVING):

Calories: 250

19.7g of total fat

7.3g of saturated fat.

226 mg of sodium a

6.7 g of carbohydrates

HEALTH BENEFIT:

A superfood, rocket is a fantastic source of calcium, the vitamins A, C, and K, as well as dietary fibre. A fantastic source of protein and good fats is goat cheese. The recipe is enhanced with flavour, nutrients, and healthy fats thanks to olive oil, balsamic vinegar, and garlic. The salad gains a crunchy texture and nutty flavour from the roasted pine nuts.

INGREDIENT ALTERNATIVES:

If you don't have a rocket, you can use baby spinach or arugula as a substitute. Goat cheese can be replaced with feta cheese. You can substitute sunflower seeds, pumpkin seeds, or slivered almonds for pine nuts if you don't have any on hand. Avocado oil or walnut oil are more options for extra-virgin olive oil.

SUMMER MELON SALAD

Prepare time 10 minutes

serve 6

INGREDIENTS:

2 small Honeydew melons, peeled, seeded, and cut into cubes

2 small Cantaloupe melons

2 tablespoons of extra-virgin olive oil

2 tablespoons of finely chopped fresh mint and basil

2 teaspoons of honey;

2 tablespoons of toasted pumpkin seeds

1/4 teaspoon of freshly ground black pepper

1/4 teaspoon of sea salt.

INSTRUCTIONS:

1. Combine the honeydew and cantaloupe melon, mint, basil, lemon juice, and olive oil in a big bowl.

2. Slowly blend by stirring.

3. Combine the honey, pumpkin seeds, pepper, and salt in a small bowl.

4. Pour the honey mixture over the melon mixture and gently stir to combine.

5. Transfer the salad to a serving bowl and serve chilled.

NUTRIENT CONTENT (PER SERVING):

Calories: 126

6.9 g of total fat

0 mg of cholesterol.

16.5 g of total carbohydrates

2.5 g of dietary fibre

11.2 g of sugars

2.2 g of protein.

HEALTH BENEFIT:

For those trying to stick to a low-cholesterol diet, this summer melon salad is a fantastic option. Honeydew and cantaloupe melons, which are both low in cholesterol and saturated fat, are the key components of this salad. They are also a great source of dietary fibre, vitamins A and C, and vitamin C, all of which help lower cholesterol and lower the risk of heart disease. Fresh herbs, olive oil, and lemon juice give the dish a flavour boost and more nutrition.

INGREDIENT ALTERNATIVES:

•You can use canned fruit in their place if fresh honeydew and cantaloupe melons are unavailable.

• Dried herbs can be used in place of fresh mint and basil if you don't have access to them.

• You can use sunflower seeds or slivered almonds in place of pumpkin seeds if you don't have any on hand. Honey can be substituted with agave nectar or maple syrup.

• Avocado or flaxseed oil are two options if you want to substitute for olive oil.

BARBEQUE TOFU SALAD

30 minutes for preparation

4 servings

INGREDIENTS:

- 400g Firm Tofu, cubed
- 4 tablespoons of Barbeque sauce
- 2 tablespoons of olive oil
- 2 tablespoons of sesame oil
- 1 small red onion, finely chopped
- 2 cloves of garlic, minced
- 2 tablespoons of freshly chopped cilantro
- 1 red bell pepper, diced
- 1 teaspoon of cumin
- 2 tablespoons of fresh lemon juice
- 2 tablespoons of fresh parsley
- 2 cups of cooked quinoa
- 2 cups of cooked black beans
- Salt and pepper to taste

INSTRUCTIONS:

1. Set oven temperature to 375 degrees Fahrenheit (190 degrees Celsius).

2. Arrange the cubed tofu on a parchment-lined baking pan.

3. Coat the tofu by drizzling it with sesame and olive oils.

4. Season the tofu with the cumin, salt, and pepper, then toss to coat.

5. Bake for 20 minutes, flipping the cubes halfway through.

6. Remove the baked tofu from the oven and allow it to cool.

7. Combine the cooked quinoa, black beans, red pepper, red onion, garlic, cilantro, and parsley in a big bowl.

8. Add the cooled tofu cubes and the barbeque sauce and toss to combine.

9. Add the lemon juice and toss the salad to mix.

10.Serve the salad at room temperature or chilled.

NUTRIENT CONTENT (PER SERVING):

Energy: 302 kcal

29g of carbohydrates

15g of protein

Fat: 16g

2.5g of saturated fat

0 mg of cholesterol

Salt: 409 mg

6.7g of fibre

HEALTH BENEFIT:

Quinoa and black beans offer an extra dose of protein and fibre, and tofu is a fantastic source of plant-based protein. Moreover, olive oil and sesame oil offer good fats that support satiety and fullness.

INGREDIENT ALTERNATIVES:

You can use pinto beans or chickpeas in place of black beans if you don't have any on hand. Another grain, like brown rice or barley, can be used in place of quinoa. You can substitute parsley for cilantro if you don't have any. Any type of oil, like olive oil or avocado oil, can be used in place of sesame oil.

Jeffery F. Maurer

DESSERT RECIPES

DESSERT RECIPES

APPLE CHEESECAKE

Prep Time: 30 minutes

Servings: 8-10

INGREDIENTS:

Two big eggs, two Granny Smith apples, peeled, cored, and diced

two tablespoons of lemon juice

two tablespoons of brown sugar

200 grammes of crushed digestive biscuits

500 grammes of low-fat cream cheese

100 grammes of caster sugar

Two teaspoons of vanilla extract.

INSTRUCTIONS:

1. Set oven temperature to 350°F (180°C). A Grease and line a 9-inch springform cake tin with parchment paper.

2. Combine the digestive scone crumbs and melted butter in a large bowl. Press the mixture firmly into the bottom of the prepared tin.

3. In another dish, combine the cream cheese, caster sugar, and vanilla extract and mix until well combined.

4. Add the eggs one at a time, beating until combined.

5. Combine the diced apples, lemon juice, and brown sugar in a small bowl.

6 Spoon half of the cream cheese mixture over the digestive biscuit base. Top with the

apple mixture, then spoon over the remaining cream cheese mixture.

7. Bake the cheesecake in a preheated oven for 25 to 30 minutes, or until it is firm.

8. Allow to cool completely before slicing and serving.

NUTRIENT CONTENT (PER SERVING):

211 kcal of calories

11.4 g of total fat,

6.7 g of saturated fat

0 g of trans fat.

55 mg of cholesterol

22.6 g of total carbohydrates

1.2 g of dietary fibre

13.5 g of sugars

4.3 g of protein.

HEALTH BENEFIT:

This dessert is a healthier option because low-fat cream cheese is used and no additional fats are added. The apples used in this recipe are also a fantastic source of antioxidants and dietary fibre, both of which can support a healthy heart.

NUTRIENT CONTENT (PER SERVING):

• If you can't find digestive biscuits, you can use graham crackers or any other kind of biscuit in their place.

• You can use 2 tablespoons of honey for the sugar if you'd prefer to do so.

• To make this dish vegan, use vegan cream cheese and a flax egg combination in place of the eggs.

KIWI FRUIT TART

Prep Time: 45 minutes

10 servings

INGREDIENTS:

Crust: 140g unbleached flour

Margarine in 60g

2 tablespoons water, ice

Filling:

2 ripe, sizable kiwis, peeled and sliced thin.

Honey, two tablespoons

5 tablespoons plain, low-fat yoghurt

Two tablespoons of cornflour.

Lemon juice, 2 teaspoons

2 teaspoons of sugar, caster

A pinch of ginger powder

INSTRUCTIONS:

1. Set the oven to 180 C (350 F).

2. Combine the margarine and plain flour in a medium bowl and stir until the mixture resembles fine breadcrumbs.

3. Stirring constantly, gradually add the cold water until the dough holds together.

4. Roll out the dough to suit a 20cm (8-inch) tart pan on a lightly dusted surface.

5. Set the tart pan on a baking sheet and use your fingers to press the dough into the bottom and sides of the pan.

6. Use a fork to prick the tart's bottom and bake for 10 minutes in the preheated oven.

7. To make the filling, combine the honey, yoghurt, cornflour, lemon juice, sugar and ginger in a medium bowl.

8. Evenly distribute the mixture over the tart's base.

9. Place the slices of kiwi fruit on top of the tart.

10. Bake the kiwi fruit in the preheated oven for 25 minutes, or until it is just beginning to brown.

11. Let the tart cool completely before slicing.

NUTRIENT CONTENT (PER SERVING):

149 calories

2.5g protein

18.4g of carbohydrates

Fat: 7.2g

2.1g of saturated fat

0 mg of cholesterol

0.9g of fibre

HEALTH BENEFIT:

the Kiwi Fruit Tart. The kiwi fruit is a fantastic source of fibre and vitamin C, both of which prevent cholesterol from being absorbed in the intestine and so lower cholesterol levels. The tart also includes honey and low-fat yoghurt, two additional natural sources of antioxidants that can help prevent heart disease and stroke.

INGREDIENT ALTERNATIVES:

• You can use a vegan-friendly spread in place of the margarine if you prefer a vegan option.

• You can use gluten-free flour in place of regular flour to make the tart gluten-free.

• Maple syrup or agave nectar can be used in place of honey if you don't have any on hand.

• You can use full-fat yoghurt to give the tart a richer flavour.

SWEETATO BUNDT CAKE

Prep Time: 15 minutes

Servings: 8

INGREDIENTS:

- 200g self-raising flour
- 2 tsp baking powder
- 1/4 tsp salt
- 1/2 tsp ground cinnamon
- Two large sweet potatoes, shredded after being peeled
- 200g caster sugar
- 3 large eggs
- 160ml vegetable oil
- 1 tsp vanilla extract
- Zest of 1 orange
- 2 tbsp freshly squeezed orange juice

• 2 tbsp chopped pecans

INSTRUCTIONS:

1. Set the oven to 180°C or 350°F. A 10-inch Bundt pan should be floured and greased before use.

2. Combine the flour, baking powder, salt, and ground cinnamon in a medium bowl.

3. Combine the grated sweet potatoes, sugar, eggs, oil, vanilla essence, orange zest, and orange juice in a separate, big basin.

4. Add the dry ingredients to the wet ingredients and mix until just combined.

5. Spoon the batter into the Bundt pan that has been prepped and sprinkle the chopped pecans over the top.

6. Bake the pie for 40 to 45 minutes, or until a toothpick inserted in the middle comes out clean.

7. After 15 minutes, turn the cake over onto a wire rack to finish cooling.

NUTRIENT CONTENT (PER SERVING):

kilocalories: 397

Fat: 14.6 g

58.4 g of carbohydrates

5.2 g of protein

2.3 g of fibre.

30.3 g of sugar

HEALTH BENEFIT:

Naturally low in fat and cholesterol and abundant in dietary fibre, vitamins, and minerals are sweet potatoes. Also, they are a rich source of complex carbs, which are crucial for preserving normal blood sugar levels. The orange juice and zest in the recipe give it an extra vitamin C boost while also adding a hint of citrus flavour. The pecans provide a crunchy texture and are a good source of heart-healthy monounsaturated fats.

INGREDIENT ALTERNATIVES:

All-purpose flour and one teaspoon of baking powder can be used as a substitute for self-raising flour if you don't have any on hand.

You can use 1/2 teaspoon of orange extract in place of orange zest and juice if you don't have any on hand.

You can use any other nut in their place, such as walnuts or almonds if you don't have pecans.

RAISIN CHOCOLATE SLICES

10 minutes for preparation

12 servings

Ingredients:

• Plain Flour, 120g (4.2 oz)

• Chocolate Powder, 30g (1.1 oz)

• Light Soft Brown Sugar, 120g (4.2 oz)

• Low-Fat Spread, 125g (4.4 oz)

• 25g (0.9 oz) of raisins • 2 teaspoons of vanilla extract

Instructions:

1. Set your oven's temperature to 180 C (350 F/Gas 4).

2. Grease a cake pan that is 20 cm (8 inches) square.

3. Combine the flour and cocoa powder in a medium bowl.

4. Add the sugar and combine.

5. Add the low-fat spread and mix until the mixture resembles breadcrumbs.

6. Add the raisins and vanilla extract, and combine until a soft dough forms.

7. Spread the dough out evenly and press it into the cake pan.

8. Bake for 25 minutes in the preheated oven.

9. Take out of the oven, then let cool in the tin.

10. Slice into 12 pieces, then serve.

NUTRIENT CONTENT (PER SERVING):

• Calories: 118.

- Fat: 4.6g
- Saturated Fat: 2.3g
- Carbohydrates: 19.3g
- Sugar: 10.2g
- Protein: 1.6g
- Fibre: 0.7g
- Sodium: 0.1g

HEALTH BENEFIT:

These cookies are a healthier option than other snacks because they contain less saturated fat and cholesterol thanks to the low-fat spread and absence of butter in the recipe. Moreover, raisins are a fantastic source of nutritional fibre, which lowers cholesterol levels.

INGREDIENT ALTERNATIVES:

You can use olive oil or olive oil in place of the low-fat spread if you want something healthier. Another option is to use a sugar alternative, such as honey or stevia, in place of the sugar. You might try other dried fruits, such as sultanas, dates, or apricots if you don't like raisins.

FRUIT YOGHURT PARFAIT

Prep Time: 15 minutes

Servings: 4

INGREDIENTS:

2 cups of Greek yoghurt.

2 tablespoons of vanilla extract

1/4 cup of honey

2 cups of fresh fruit (such as blueberries, strawberries, raspberries, etc.)

Two tablespoons each of chopped almonds and grated coconut

NUTRIENT CONTENT (PER SERVING):

223 calories

Protein is 7.5g,

fat is 5.5g,

carbohydrates are 35g

fibre is 3.5g.

0 mg of cholesterol

INSTRUCTIONS:

1. Combine the Greek yoghurt, honey, and vanilla essence in a medium bowl. Blend thoroughly, then set aside.

2. Choose the fresh fruit of your choosing, such as blueberries, strawberries, raspberries, etc., then wash and prepare it.

3. In four individual glasses or bowls, layer the yoghurt mixture, fresh fruit and chopped almonds and shredded coconut.

4. Serve cold and take pleasure!

HEALTH BENEFIT:

A parfait of fruit and yoghurt makes a great low-cholesterol snack or dessert. Although almonds and coconut contribute healthy fats and extra crunch, fresh fruit and Greek yoghurt supply vital vitamins and minerals. Moreover, this dish has a lot of fibre, a vitamin crucial for preserving a good cholesterol level.

INGREDIENT ALTERNATIVES:

• To make a vegan version, use a vegan yoghurt substitute in place of the Greek yoghurt.

• You can use maple syrup or agave nectar for honey if you don't have any on hand.

• You can substitute walnuts or pecans for almonds if you don't have any on hand.

• You can use chopped dried fruit like raisins or dried cranberries if you don't have coconut that has been shredded.

CASHEW BUTTER LATTE

10 minutes for preparation

1 serving

INGREDIENTS:

1/2 cup cashew milk

2 tablespoons cashew butter

1 tablespoon honey

1/4 teaspoon ground cardamom

1 shot of espresso.

Optional: Vanilla extract, 1 teaspoon

INSTRUCTIONS:

1. Heat the cashew milk in a medium saucepan over medium-high heat until it is warm but not boiling.

2. Add the cashew butter, honey, cinnamon, and cardamom and stir until the cashew butter is melted and all the ingredients are combined.

3. Turn off the heat and pour the mixture into a mug.

4. Brew the espresso and add to the mug.

5. Add the vanilla extract, if preferred.

6. Combine by stirring, then savour!

NUTRIENT CONTENT (PER SERVING):

Energy: 418 kcal

28.9g of carbohydrates

6.6g of protein

Fat: 29.6g

4.2g of saturated fat

0.9g of fibre

24.2g sugar

HEALTH BENEFIT:

this Cashew Butter Latte is a terrific way to satisfy your caffeine craving. Healthy fats, proteins, and minerals like magnesium, phosphorus, and zinc can all be found in cashew butter. Honey is a healthy natural sweetener with anti-inflammatory and antioxidant qualities. Cinnamon is a potent antioxidant that can help lower blood sugar levels and reduce inflammation. Cardamom is a warming spice that has long been employed in folk medicine. Last but not least, espresso is a fantastic source of antioxidants and can enhance cognitive performance.

INGREDIENT ALTERNATIVES:

If you don't have cashew milk, you can use almond or oat milk or any other plant-based milk.

If you don't have cashew butter, you can use almond or peanut butter, or any other nut butter.

If you don't have honey, you can substitute agave nectar or maple syrup.

If you don't have espresso, use freshly brewed coffee instead.

In place of cardamom, you can substitute nutmeg or ginger.

CHOCOLATE CHIP BANANA MUFFINS

10 minutes for preparation

12 servings

INGREDIENTS:

180 grammes of plain flour

one teaspoon of baking powder

½ teaspoons of bicarbonate of soda

a dash of salt

75ml of vegetable oil

75g of soft light brown sugar

1 egg.

2 mashed, ripe bananas

Chocolate Chips, 75g

Instructions:

1. Set the oven's temperature to 190 C (375 F, gas mark 5). Line a 12-hole muffin tin with paper muffin cases.

2. Pour the salt, baking soda, flour, baking powder, and flour into a large bowl and set aside.

3. Combine the egg, oil, and sugar in another bowl by beating them just until incorporated.

4. Add the mashed banana and blend with the egg mixture.

5. To add the wet components, create a well in the middle of the dry ingredients. Mix until just combined. Be careful not to over mix.

6. Carefully incorporate the chocolate chips.

7. Divide the mixture between the muffin cases, filling each case to two-thirds full.

8. Bake for 15-20 minutes in a preheated oven, or until a skewer inserted in the centre of a muffin comes out clean.

9. After 5 minutes, allow the cake to cool in the mould before transferring it to a wire rack to finish cooling.

NUTRIENT CONTENT (PER SERVING):

136 kcal of energy

Protein: 2.1 grammes

20.5g of carbohydrates

9.4g are sugars.

Fat – 5.1g

0.7g of fibre

0.2g of sodium

HEALTH BENEFIT:

these chocolate chip banana muffins are a terrific way to fulfill a sweet desire. The muffins' inherent sweetness is increased by the banana, while flavour and texture are added by the chocolate chips. This dish uses vegetable oil instead of butter since it lowers the amount of cholesterol and saturated fat that butter contains. In addition, the banana's fibre contributes to longer-lasting satiety.

INGREDIENT ALTERNATIVES:

- Self-raising flour can be substituted for ordinary flour if you don't have any, and baking soda and bicarbonate of soda can be left out.

- You can use olive oil in its place if you don't have any vegetable oil.

- You can substitute caster sugar for soft light brown sugar if you don't have any.

- You can use chopped nuts or dried fruit for the chocolate chips if you don't have any on hand.

FISH AND SEA FOOD

FISH AND SEAFOOD

RED SNAPPER SCAMPI

Prep Time: 15 minutes

Servings: 4

INGREDIENTS:

• 4 Red Snapper fillets, weighing approximately 150g each

• 2 tablespoons olive oil

• 2 tablespoons butter

• 2 cloves garlic, minced

• 1 small shallot, minced

• 2 tablespoons white wine

• 2 tablespoons freshly squeezed lemon juice

• 2 tablespoons fresh parsley, chopped

• 1 teaspoon sea salt

• 1/4 teaspoon freshly ground black pepper

INSTRUCTIONS:

1. Set the oven's temperature 176°C.

2. Place the red snapper fillets on a parchment-lined baking sheet. Olive oil and salt and pepper are sprinkled over the fillets.

3. Bake the fish for 8 to 10 minutes, or until it is well done.

4. Meanwhile, heat the butter in a large skillet over medium heat. Add the garlic and shallot and sauté until fragrant, about 2 minutes.

5. Stir in the white wine and lemon juice, and cook for 3 to 4 minutes, or until the sauce has somewhat reduced.

6. Add the parsley, salt and pepper and stir to combine. Turn off the heat

7. Arrange the red snapper fillets that have been fried on a serving platter. Spoon the sauce over the fish.

NUTRIENT CONTENT (PER SERVING):

277 calories

Fat: 13.3g

2.1g of carbohydrates

29.2g of protein

Salt: 705 mg

65mg of cholesterol

HEALTH BENEFIT:

Red snapper is a lean protein source that is high in lean nutrients and has few calories. It also contains a lot of Omega-3 fatty acids, which might improve cardiovascular health and lessen inflammation. Red snapper is also a high source of selenium and vitamin B12, both of which are necessary for normal nerve and brain function. Olive oil, garlic, and lemon juice combine to provide a tasty, nutrient-rich sauce that is low in cholesterol and can assist the food's health advantages.

INGREDIENT ALTERNATIVES:

If red snapper is not available, you can substitute any other firm-fleshed white fish, such as cod or halibut. White wine can be substituted with dry white vermouth or chicken broth if you can't locate any. For a dairy-free alternative, you can alternatively use vegan butter or olive oil in place of the butter.

Jeffery F. Maurer

GRILLED SCALLOPS WITH GREMOLATA

15 minutes for preparation

2 servings

INGREDIENTS:

12 large scallops

2 tablespoons of extra virgin olive oil

2 chopped garlic cloves

two teaspoons of freshly cut parsley

two tablespoons of lemon juice

a dash of salt and freshly ground black pepper, to taste

one teaspoon of shredded lemon zest

Nutrient Content (Per Serving):

208 calories

Fat: 11 g

6 g of carbohydrates

18 g of protein

Salt: 166 mg

83 mg of cholesterol

Instructions:

1. Preheat your grill to medium-high heat.

2. Combine the lemon juice, lemon zest, parsley, garlic, and olive oil in a small bowl. Mix together until combined.

3. Place the scallops in a shallow dish and pour the olive oil mixture over them. Gently turn the scallops to coat them in the mixture.

4. Add the scallops to the grill that has been heated. Cook each side for two minutes.

5. Take the scallops from the grill and give them a taste-testing sprinkle of salt and pepper.

6. Serve the scallops with the gremolata. Enjoy!

HEALTH BENEFIT:

Enjoying seafood in the form of this dish of grilled scallops with gremolata is delectable and nutritious. Essential elements like protein, selenium, and omega-3 fatty acids are present in the scallops. The gremolata contains extra vitamins and minerals thanks to olive oil, garlic, and lemon juice. Scallops with gremolata are a fantastic choice for a low-cholesterol diet because they are low in cholesterol and high in beneficial fats.

INGREDIENT ALTERNATIVES:

You can substitute prawn or squid for the huge scallops if you can't find them. Canola oil or vegetable oil can also be used in place of olive oil. If you don't have any fresh parsley, you can substitute dried. Finally, you can use bottled lemon juice if you don't have any fresh lemon juice.

SHRIMP AND PINEAPPLE LETTUCE WRAPS

10 minutes for preparation

4 servings

INGREDIENTS:

1 large pineapple, diced

250g cooked, peeled shrimo

2 tablespoons olive oil

2 tablespoons freshly squeezed lime juice

4 large iceberg lettuce leaves

2 tablespoons chopped fresh cilantro

2 tablespoons diced red onion

1 teaspoon honey

1/2 teaspoon sea salt

1/4 teaspoon powdered black pepper

INSTRUCTIONS:

1. Combine the shrimp, pineapple, lime juice, red onion, honey, salt, and pepper in a medium bowl.

2. Combine everything by mixing it all.

3. Lay the lettuce leaves on a plate and spoon the shrimp and pineapple mixture onto the center of each leaf.

4. Add cilantro and then serve.

NUTRIENT CONTENT (PER SERVING):

197 calories

17.2 g of carbohydrates

11.9g of protein

Fat: 8.2g

2.3g of fibre

532 milligrammes of sodium

HEALTH BENEFIT:

Shrimp and pineapple lettuce wraps are a terrific low-cholesterol supper option. The prawn is a rich source of phosphorus, selenium, and vitamin B12 and is a lean source of protein. Manganese, dietary fibre, and vitamin C are all abundant in pineapple. Olive oil contains heart-healthy lipids, while lime juice is a good source of vitamin C. The lettuce leaves are an excellent source of fibre and vitamin A.

INGREDIENT EXCHANGES:

If you don't have shrimp, you can use cubed chicken or tofu as a substitute. Papaya or mango dice can be used as a substitute for pineapple if you don't have any. You can use diced shallot or green onion as a replacement if you don't have red onion. If you don't have any cilantro, you can use mint or parsley that has just been cut.

VIETNAMESE FISH AND NOODLE BOWL

Prep time: 15 minutes

Servings: 4

INGREDIENTS:

• 4 fillets of fresh cod fish, skinless, 4 ounces each

• 2 tablespoons of soy sauce

• 2 tablespoons of vegetable oil

• 1 tablespoon of sesame oil

• 2 tablespoons of rice vinegar

• 2 teaspoons of honey

• 2 cloves of garlic, minced

• 2 teaspoons of grated ginger

• 1 teaspoon of sesame seeds

• 2 tablespoons of chopped fresh cilantro

- 2 tablespoons of chopped scallions
- 4 ounces of thin rice noodles
- 2 cups of bean sprouts
- 2 cups of shredded carrots
- 2 tablespoons of freshly chopped basil
- 2 tablespoons of freshly chopped mint
- 2 tablespoons of freshly chopped Thai basil
- 2 tablespoons of freshly chopped cilantro

INSTRUCTIONS:

1. Set the oven's temperature to 300 Celsius

2. Arrange cod fillets on a parchment-lined baking sheet.

3. Combine soy sauce, sesame oil, rice vinegar, honey, garlic, ginger, and sesame seeds in a small bowl.

4. Bake the cod fillets for 10 to 15 minutes, or until the fish is thoroughly done.

5. In the meantime, prepare the rice noodles as directed on the package.

6. Combine cooked noodles, bean sprouts, carrots, cilantro, mint, and Thai basil in a big bowl.

7. Divide the noodle mixture into 4 bowls.

8. Add a cod fillet and scallions to the top of each bowl.

NUTRIENT CONTENT (PER SERVING):

241 calories

Fat: 8.2g

28.5g of carbohydrates.

14.3g of protein

Salt: 470 mg

HEALTH BENEFIT:

The omega-3 fatty acids found in fish are a rich source of lean protein and have been demonstrated to lower cholesterol levels. A good amount of dietary fibre, which also lowers cholesterol levels, is found in fresh veggies. The rice noodles are an excellent source of complex carbs and a low-calorie substitute for regular pasta.

INGREDIENT ALTERNATIVES:

• Salmon or tilapia are additional lean proteins that can be used in place of cod fish.

•Tamari or liquid aminos can be used in place of soy sauce.

• Soba or udon noodles, as well as other varieties of noodles, can be used in place of rice noodles.

• Alfalfa or mung bean sprouts, for example, can be used in place of bean sprouts.

• Sesame oil can be substituted with other types of oil such as canola or olive oil.

• Dried herbs can be used in place of fresh herbs.

SALMON WITH FARRO PILAF

10 minutes for preparation

Time to cook: 20 minutes

4 servings

INGREDIENTS:

2 cups low-sodium vegetable broth

1 cup diced fresh tomatoes

4 (6-ounce) salmon fillets

2 tablespoons extra-virgin olive oil

1 teaspoon sea salt

1 teaspoon freshly ground black pepper

2 tablespoons of freshly squeezed lemon juice

1/4 cup minced fresh parsley

1/2 cup sliced red bell pepper.

INSTRUCTIONS:

1. Set the oven to 375°F.

2. Place the salmon fillets on a baking sheet and brush with 1 tablespoon of the olive oil. Sprinkle with the salt and pepper.

3. Bake the salmon for 20 minutes, or until it is done.

4. In the meantime, warm up the last tablespoon of olive oil in a big pot over medium heat. Add the farro and cook, stirring often, for 3 minutes.

5. Add the veggie broth and bring the mixture to a boil. Reduce the heat to low and simmer, covered, for 15 minutes..

6. Continue to boil the farro for an additional 5 minutes after adding the tomatoes, bell pepper, and parsley.

7. Turn the heat off and add the lemon juice.

8. Serve the salmon with the farro pilaf.

NUTRIENT CONTENT (PER SERVING):

372 calories

Fat: 11g

34.5g of carbohydrates

28.5g of protein

57mg of cholesterol

522 mg of sodium

HEALTH BENEFIT:

Farro, which is used in this recipe, is a wonderful source of dietary fibre, which can lower cholesterol levels and possibly aid in weight loss. Vitamins, minerals, and antioxidants from tomatoes, bell pepper, and parsley aid to lessen inflammation and advance general health.

INGREDIENT ALTERNATIVES:

- Quinoa, bulgur, or brown rice can all be used in place of farro.

- Tofu or tempeh can be used in place of the salmon to make this recipe vegan.

- Replace the farro in the recipe with quinoa or brown rice to make it gluten-free.

HADDOCK TACOS WITH SPICY SLAW

15 minutes for preparation
4 servings

INGREDIENTS:

Haddock fillets weighing 500 grammes

4 tablespoons of olive oil

2 teaspoons of cumin

2 teaspoons of garlic powder

2-tablespoons of paprika

1 teaspoon black pepper, ground

2 juiced limes

Mayonnaise, 2 tablespoons

Natural yoghurt, 2 teaspoons

2 teaspoons of pepper flakes

2 tablespoons finely chopped coriander

200g finely shredded cabbage

1 red onion

8 white corn tortillas

INSTRUCTIONS:

1. Set the oven's temperature to 200°C (400°F).

2 Haddock fillets should be placed on a baking sheet and brushed with olive oil.

3. Combine the cumin, paprika, paprika powder, and black pepper, and combine. sprinkle this over the haddock.

4. To fully cook the haddock, bake it in the oven for 8 to 10 minutes.

5. In the meantime, combine the coriander, mayonnaise, yoghurt, lime juice, and chilli powder in a dish.

6. Add the onion and cabbage to the bowl and stir to evenly distribute the dressing.

7. Heat the tortillas in a dry pan over a medium heat until they are warm and soft.

8. Cut the haddock into 8 equal pieces, and then put one on each tortilla.

9. Add some of the hot slaws on the top of each taco before serving.

NUTRIENT CONTENT (PER SERVING):

390 calories.

25.5g of protein

19.1g of fat

26.1g of carbohydrates

4.3g of fibre.

HEALTH BENEFIT:

Haddock is a low-fat protein source, making it a great choice for anyone trying to manage their cholesterol. Moreover, it contains omega-3 fatty acids, which are good for your general health. This dish also contains a lot of nutritional fibre, which helps to maintain a healthy digestive tract and control blood sugar levels. The slaw is a fantastic source of vitamins and minerals, and the spices used in this dish provide flavour without adding calories.

INGREDIENT ALTERNATIVES:

- If haddock is not available, you may substitute any other white fish.
- You can substitute your favourite herbs and spices for those specified if you don't have any of them on hand.

- Any other sort of crunchy vegetable, such as carrots or bell peppers, may be used in place of the cabbage.

- You are free to use whichever tortilla you like, including gluten-free, wheat, or corn tortillas.

STEAMED SOLE ROLLS WITH GREENS

15 minutes for preparation

4 servings

INGREDIENTS:

• 4 (4-ounce) freshly prepared sole fillets

• One teaspoon of olive oil

• 1 tsp.freshly squeezed lemon juice

Baby spinach, 4 ounces

• 4 ounces of Swiss chard, diced with the stems removed.

• 2 tablespoons of finely chopped flat-leaf parsley.

• 2 tablespoons of fresh dill, chopped finely.

• White wine, 2 teaspoons

Freshly grated Parmesan cheese, two tablespoons

Add salt and freshly ground black pepper to taste.

• Eight thin prosciutto slices

• Butter, two tablespoons

• Water, 2 tablespoons

•Serving-size lemon wedges

NUTRIENT CONTENT (PER SERVING):

153 calories

2g carbs

15g of protein

Fat: 8.4g

3.3g of saturated fat

45 mg. cholesterol

360 mg of sodium

INSTRUCTIONS:

1. After rinsing, dry the sole fillets with paper towels.

2. Combine the spinach, Swiss chard, parsley, dill, white wine, Parmesan cheese, salt, and pepper in a medium bowl with olive oil, lemon juice, and other ingredients. Stir everything together completely.

3. Place a sole fillet on a cutting board and top with one-eighth of the spinach mixture. Roll up the fillet and wrap it tightly with a slice of prosciutto. Repeat with the remaining fillets and spinach mixture.

4. In a big skillet, heat the water and butter over medium-high heat. Add the rolls and

cook for about 4 minutes, turning occasionally, until the prosciutto is crisp and the sole is cooked through.

5. Serve the rolls with lemon wedges.

INGREDIENT ALTERNATIVES:

• You can substitute any other white fish fillet, such as cod or snapper if you don't have sole fillets.

• You may substitute kale, spinach, or arugula for Swiss chard if you don't have any on hand.

• Gruyere or Pecorino Romano cheese can be substituted for Parmesan if you don't have any.

• Bacon or ham can be substituted for prosciutto if you don't have any.

HEALTH BENEFIT:

The sole fillets are minimal in fat and calories and a great source of lean protein. The Parmesan cheese and olive oil give healthy fats and a wonderful flavour, while the dark leafy greens are full of vitamins, minerals, and antioxidants. Without significantly increasing the amount of fat or cholesterol, the prosciutto adds a salty, smokey flavour. With this dish, you may have a flavorful and filling supper without worrying about your cholesterol levels.

LEMON GARLIC MACKEREL

4 servings

10 minutes for preparation

ingredients:

• 4 mackerel, cleaned and filleted

• 2 cloves garlic, minced

• 2 tablespoons fresh lemon juice

• 2 tablespoons olive oil

• Salt and pepper to taste

• 2 tablespoons fresh parsley, chopped

• 1 teaspoon crushed dried oregano

• 2 tablespoons chopped fresh dill

INSTRUCTIONS:

1. Set oven to 400 degrees Fahrenheit (200 degrees C).

2. In a shallow baking dish, arrange mackerel fillets in a single layer.

3. Combine the garlic, lemon juice, olive oil, salt, and pepper in a small bowl.

4. Pour the mixture on top of the mackerel.

5. Sorinkle with dill, oregano, and parsley.

6. Bake the fish for 10 minutes, or until it is thoroughly cooked and the top is just beginning to brown.

NUTRIENT CONTENT (PER SERVING):

• 222 kcal of calories

• Cholesterol: 66 mg

• Total Fat: 14.3 g

• Saturated Fat: 2.1 g

1.3 g of total carbohydrate

0.5 g of dietary fibre

0.3 g of sugars

22.5 g of protein.

HEALTH BENEFIT:

Omega-3 fatty acids, which are vital for cardiovascular health, are abundant in mackerel. Garlic and herbs offer taste and nutrients, while fresh lemon juice and olive oil add flavour and healthy fats. This dish is a terrific way to consume a nutritious meal because it is minimal in calories and cholesterol.

INGREDIENT ALTERNATIVES:

You can substitute any other sort of fish, such as salmon, cod, or tilapia if you don't have mackerel. Canola oil or any kind of vegetable oil can also be used in place of olive oil. You can substitute dried herbs if you don't have any fresh ones. If preferred, you can instead use lime or vinegar in place of the lemon juice.

SPICY CATFISH TACOS

30 minutes for preparation

Servings: yields four tacos.

INGREDIENTS:

• 4 catfish fillets (about 120g each), skinless

• 2 tablespoons olive oil

• 1 teaspoon ground cumin

• 1 teaspoon smoked paprika

• 1 teaspoon garlic powder

• ½ teaspoon onion powder

• ½ teaspoon dried oregano

• ½ teaspoon sea salt

• 4 whole-wheat flour tortillas (about 20cm in diameter)

• 2 avocados, peeled, pitted and sliced

• 2 cups shredded lettuce

- 2 tomatoes, diced
- 1 lime, cut into 4 wedges
- 2 tablespoons of fresh cilantro, chopped
- 2 tablespoons of plain Greek yoghurt
- 2 tablespoons of salsa

INSTRUCTIONS:

1. Set the oven to 200 C.

2. Combine olive oil, cumin, smoked paprika, garlic, onion, oregano, and sea salt in a small bowl.

3. Arrange catfish fillets on a parchment-lined baking pan. Brush the spice mixture on each fillet.

4. Bake for 15-20 minutes in a preheated oven, or until the fish is cooked through and flakes readily.

5. Warm the tortillas in the oven for 5 minutes, or until they are just beginning to turn golden.

6. To assemble the tacos, place one catfish fillet onto each warm tortilla. Top with avocado slices, lettuce, tomatoes, lime wedges and cilantro.

7. Top with salsa and Greek yoghurt. Serve right away.

NUTRIENT CONTENT (PER SERVING):

345 calories

Fat: 11g

33g of carbohydrates

24g of protein

535 milligrammes of sodium

HEALTH BENEFIT:

The catfish is a low-saturated-fat, lean source of protein that is a great option for persons with high cholesterol. While the spices give flavour without adding too much sodium, the use of olive oil in the dish helps to improve the number of good fats. The addition of avocado, lettuce, tomatoes, and lime wedges makes the meal even healthier by adding more vitamins, minerals, and fibre.

INGREDIENT ALTERNATIVES:

You can substitute any other firm white fish, such as cod, haddock, or tilapia if you don't have catfish. The whole-wheat tortillas can be swapped out for corn tortillas or lettuce wraps. Use a pre-made taco seasoning mix if you don't have any of the stated spices. You can use sour cream or vegan mayonnaise for Greek yoghurt. Last but not least, you can substitute diced tomatoes and a dash of chilli powder if you don't have any salsa.

CITRUS COD BAKE

20 minutes for preparation

4 servings

INGREDIENTS:

 4 fillets of cod (roughly 150g each)

- 2 tablespoons of olive oil - 2 lemons' juice

- 2 minced garlic cloves

- 2 teaspoons finely chopped fresh thyme

- 2 teaspoons freshly chopped parsley

- 2 teaspoons finely chopped fresh dill

- To taste, add salt and pepper

- 1 lemon, thinly sliced

- 200g halved cherry tomatoes

INSTRUCTIONS:

1. Set the oven's temperature to 200 °C (400 °F).

2. Put the fish fillets in a baking dish that has been buttered.

3. Combine the olive oil, lemon juice, garlic, thyme, parsley, dill, salt, and pepper in a small bowl.

4. Pour the mixture over the cod fillets and top with the lemon slices and cherry tomatoes.

5. Bake for 15-20 minutes in a preheated oven, or until the veggies are soft and the cod is thoroughly cooked.

NUTRIENT CONTENT (PER SERVING):

Energy: 243 kcal

Fat: 10.9 g

Protein: 29.5 g Carbohydrates: 5.3 g

Salt: 43 mg

68 mg of cholesterol

HEALTH BENEFIT:

Cod is a heart-healthy fish that is lean, low in fat, high in protein, and rich in omega-3 fatty acids. Lemon and herbs are added to the dish to help with flavouring and to add antioxidants and other minerals. The vitamin C in cherry tomatoes is a wonderful supply for the body and helps to lessen inflammation.

INGREDIENT ALTERNATIVES:

If you don't have cod, you can substitute another lean white fish, like haddock or tilapia. You can use dried herbs as a substitute if you don't have any fresh ones. Lemon juice can be substituted with lime juice. You can use other varieties of tomatoes, such as Roma tomatoes if you don't have cherry tomatoes.

FRIED MAHI-MAHI

10 minutes for preparation

4 servings

INGREDIENTS:

4 Mahi Mahi fillets (approx. 1 kg)

Olive oil, 2 tablespoons

Freshly squeezed lemon juice, 2 tablespoons

2 finely minced garlic cloves

1 teaspoon salt, sea

One teaspoon of freshly ground black pepper

2 teaspoons freshly chopped parsley

butter, 2 tablespoons

INSTRUCTIONS:

1. Set the oven's temperature to 200 C/400 F.

2. Place the Mahi-Mahi fillets on a baking tray and drizzle with the olive oil and lemon juice. Sprinkle with the garlic, salt, and pepper.

3. Bake for 10 minutes in the preheated oven.

4. In the meantime, heat up a big skillet with the butter over medium heat.

5. Place the Mahi-Mahi fillets in the skillet and cook for 3 minutes on each side, or until the fish is well cooked and golden brown.

6. Finish by adding some fresh parsley before serving.

NUTRIENT CONTENT (PER SERVING):

180 kilocalories

11 g total fat

4 g of saturated fat

65 mg of cholesterol

Salt: 370 mg

1 g of carbohydrates

0 g of fibre

18 g of protein

HEALTH BENEFIT:

When compared to other fried recipes, this recipe for Fried Mahi-Mahi is a fantastic way to enjoy a wonderful meal with far less cholesterol. Mahi-Mahi is a fantastic option for anyone trying to lower their cholesterol levels due to its low cholesterol content. Olive oil helps to lower the quantity of saturated fat in the dish, while lemon juice gives it a delightful taste boost.

INGREDIENT ALTERNATIVES:

You can use any other fish fillet if you don't have any mahi mahi on hand. In addition, you can swap out the olive oil for another oil, like olive oil. Use vegan butter in place of conventional butter for a dairy-free variation. Other fresh herbs, like thyme or oregano, can also be used in place of fresh parsley.

Jeffery F. Maurer

Jeffery F. Maurer

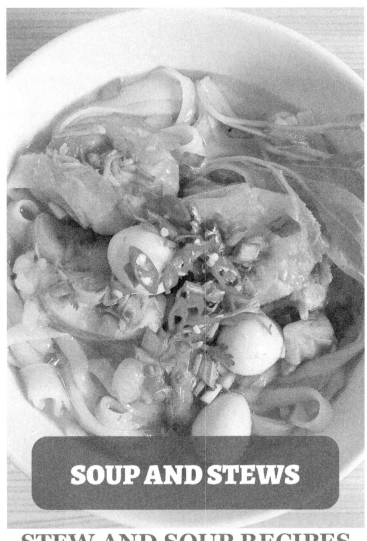

SOUP AND STEWS

STEW AND SOUP RECIPES

249

Jeffery F. Maurer

INDIAN VEGETABLE SOUP

10 minutes for preparation

Time to Cook: 25 minutes

4 servings

INGREDIENTS

- 1 tablespoon of vegetable oil

- 1 onion, diced

- 1 teaspoon of minced garlic

- 1 teaspoon of ground cumin

- 1 teaspoon of ground coriander

- 1 teaspoon of garam masala

- 1 teaspoon of ground turmeric

- 1/2 teaspoon of ground black pepper

- 1/2 teaspoon of chili powder

- 1/2 teaspoon of sea salt

- 2 cups of diced potatoes

- 2 cups of diced carrots

- 2 cups of diced tomatoes

- 2 cups of vegetable broth

- 1 can of coconut milk

- 2 tablespoons of freshly chopped cilantro

INSTRUCTIONS

1. In a big pot, heat the vegetable oil over medium heat.

2. Add the onion and garlic and sauté for 3 minutes

3. Add the sea salt, black pepper, chilli powder, turmeric, cumin, coriander, and garam masala. While constantly stirring, cook for one minute.

4. Add the coconut milk, tomatoes, potatoes, carrots, and vegetable broth. Bring to a boil, then reduce the heat to low and simmer for 15 minutes.

5. Stir in the cilantro after removing it from the heat.

NUTRIENT CONTENT (PER SERVING):

170 calories

8 g of total fat.

5 g of saturated fat

0 mg of cholesterol

Salt: 375 mg

20 g of total carbohydrates

4 g of dietary fibre

4 g of protein

HEALTH BENEFIT:

This recipe's savoury spices are loaded with antioxidants and anti-inflammatory characteristics that can help the body heal from inflammation and strengthen the immune system. This meal is a fantastic option for individuals trying to lower their levels of harmful cholesterol because it contains foods that have low cholesterol. Because of the abundance of vitamins and minerals in the fresh veggies, this soup is a fantastic source of nutrition. This soup has a lot of flavours thanks to the combination of veggies and spices, which can make it a satisfying dinner.

INGREDIENT ALTERNATIVES:

• You can substitute olive oil or any other cooking oil of your choice if you don't have vegetable oil.

• You can use any combination of spices to make up for the lack of cumin, coriander, garam masala, turmeric, black pepper, or chilli powder.

• You can substitute almond milk or any other milk of your choice if you don't have canned coconut milk.

• Parsley or any other fresh herb of your choice can be used in place of fresh cilantro.

AUBERGINE STEW

Prep time: 30 minutes

4 servings

INGREDIENTS:

• 2 large aubergines, diced into 2 cm cubes (about 500 g)

• 2 red onions, diced (about 200 g)

• 2 cloves of garlic, chopped

• 2 tablespoons of olive oil

• 1 teaspoon of cumin

• 1 teaspoon of coriander

• 2 tablespoons of tomato purée

• 2 tablespoons of freshly chopped parsley

• 400 ml of vegetable stock

• Salt and pepper, to taste

INSTRUCTIONS:

1. Turn on the oven's 200°C setting.

2.Place the diced aubergines on a baking sheet lined with parchment paper and sprinkle with 1 tablespoon of olive oil, salt and pepper. Roast in the oven for 15 minutes..

3. In the meantime, warm the rest of the olive oil in a skillet over medium heat.

4. Add the diced onions and garlic, and simmer for about 5 minutes, or until the onions start to soften.

5. Add the tomato purée, cumin, and coriander, and simmer for an additional 2 minutes.

6. Add the parsley, vegetable stock, and roasted aubergines. Bring to a boil.

7. Lower the heat and simmer the aubergines for 10 minutes, or until they are fully cooked.

8. To taste, add salt and pepper to the dish.

NUTRIENT CONTENT (PER SERVING):

Calories: 174 kcal l

9.3 g of total fat

1.3 g of saturated fat

19.3 g of carbohydrate

3.7 g of protein

717 mg of sodium

5.8 g of fibre

HEALTH BENEFIT:

With only a little amount of saturated fat, this aubergine stew is a fantastic option for individuals consuming a low-cholesterol diet. Dietary fibre, which has been demonstrated to help lower cholesterol levels, is present in abundance in aubergines. In addition, this stew is rich in vitamins and minerals including magnesium and vitamin C.

INGREDIENT ALTERNATIVES:

If you don't have aubergines on hand, you can use other vegetables instead, including mushrooms, bell peppers, or zucchini. Instead of cumin and coriander, you can instead add other herbs and spices like oregano or thyme. You can add cooked chickpeas or lentils to this stew.

CHIPOTLE BUTTERNUT SOUP

Prep time: 15 minutes

4 servings

INGREDIENTS:

Olive oil, two tablespoons

1 sliced onion

2 minced garlic cloves

3 cups diced and peeled butternut squash

5 cups vegetable broth

2 tablespoons chopped fresh cilantro,

1 teaspoon each of ground cumin, chipotle chile powder, salt

1/2 cup half-and-half

¼ tsp pepper;

Greek yoghurt plain, fresh cilantro minced, and shredded cheese are optional garnishes.

INSTRUCTIONS:

1. In a big pot over medium-high heat, warm the olive oil. Add the onion and garlic, and simmer, stirring periodically, for about 5 minutes, or until the onion is softened and just starting to brown.

2. Add the butternut squash, cumin, chili powder, salt, and pepper and stir to combine. Cook for another 2 minutes.

3. Add the veggie broth and bring the mixture to a boil. Reduce the heat to medium-low and simmer, uncovered, for 10 minutes or until the squash is tender.

4. Turn off the heat and let the pot cool a little. Blend the soup in batches in a blender

or food processor, or with an immersion blender.

5. Return the soup to the pot and stir in the half-and-half. Simmer for 5 minutes.

6. Serve the soup and top with any desired garnishes.

NUTRIENT CONTENT (PER SERVING):

132 calories

Fat: 6.3 g

15.5 g of carbohydrates, 3.2 g of protein

556.4 mg. of sodium

2.7 g of fibre

HEALTH BENEFIT:

this chipotle butternut soup is amonh the ideal recipes for a low-cholesterol diet. Healthy fats are provided by olive oil and vegetable broth, while the butternut squash is a wonderful source of fibre and vitamin A. The chipotle chile powder offers a smoky taste without adding bad fats or cholesterol, while the garlic and cumin add flavour and anti-inflammatory properties.

INGREDIENT ALTERNATIVES:

You can use an equal amount of ordinary chilli powder in its stead if you don't have any chipotle chilli powder on hand. For a dairy-free alternative, you can instead use coconut milk or almond milk in place of the half-and-half. Last but not least, feel free to use any variety of onions you have on hand, including sweet, red, or yellow onions.

CREAMY VEGETABLE SOUP

15 minutes for preparation

Time to Cook: 25 minutes

4 servings

INGREDIENTS:

2 tablespoons olive oil

1 diced onion

2 minced garlic cloves

500 grammes each of diced potatoes, carrots, and celery.

4 cups vegetable broth

1 teaspoon each of dried thyme, oregano, oregano, basil

2 bay leaves

1/4 cup of heavy cream

salt, and freshly ground black pepper to taste

a garnish of chopped fresh parsley.

INSTRUCTIONS:

1. In a big pot set over medium heat, warm the olive oil.

2. Add the onion and garlic and simmer for about 5 minutes, or until tender.

3. Add the bay leaves, thyme, oregano, basil, potatoes, carrots, celery, and vegetable broth.

4. Bring to a boil, reduce heat and simmer until the vegetables are tender, about 20 minutes.

5. Take out and throw away the bay leaves.

6. Puree the soup with an immersion blender until it is smooth.

7. Add the cream and salt and pepper to taste.

8. Garnish with fresh parsley before serving.

NUTRIENT CONTENT (PER SERVING):

170 calories

Fat: 8g

3g of saturated fat

22g of carbohydrates

4g of fibre

3g. protein

Salt: 380 mg

HEALTH BENEFIT:

The ideal dinner that is low in cholesterol is this creamy vegetable soup. The ingredients used to make this soup are rich in dietary fibre and include important vitamins and minerals like iron, potassium, vitamin c, and vitamin a. The high fibre content aids in lowering the body's harmful cholesterol levels and aids in weight management. The soup is also a fantastic source of antioxidants, which aid in the body's defence against free radicals and lower the risk of chronic illnesses.

INGREDIENT ALTERNATIVES:

• olive oil or any other vegetable oil can be used in place of olive oil.

• Almond milk or coconut cream that hasn't been sweetened can be used in place of heavy cream.

Potatoes can be substituted with sweet potatoes.

• Parsnips or turnips can be substituted for carrots.

Celery can be swapped out for fennel.

• Beef or chicken broth can be used in place of vegetable broth.

VEGGIE CHICKEN SOUP

30 minutes to prepare

8 servings.

INGREDIENTS:

Olive oil, one tablespoon

1 diced onion

2 minced garlic cloves

1 chopped red bell pepper

Diced carrots: 2

2 diced celery stalks

two cups of vegetable broth

1 (15-ounce can of drained corn

1 (14-ounce) can of chopped tomatoes

1 (15-ounce) can wash and drained black beans

2 cups chopped cooked chicken

One teaspoon of dried oregano

six ounces of frozen spinach

1 teaspoon dried basil

To taste, salt & pepper

NUTRIENT CONTENT (PER SERVING):

Calories: 257 kcal

Carbohydrates: 32 g

Protein: 20 g

Fat: 7 g

Cholesterol: 27 mg;

Fiber: 8 g;

Sugar: 8 g

INSTRUCTIONS:

1. In a big pot set over medium heat, warm the olive oil.

2. Stir in the onion, garlic, bell pepper, carrots, and celery, and cook for 5 minutes.

3. Add tomato, corn, black beans, chicken, spinach, oregano, and basil in addition to the vegetable broth. Bring to a boil and reduce heat to low. Simmer for 10 minutes, stirring occasionally.

4. After taking the pan from the heat, season to taste with salt and pepper. Serve hot.

HEALTH BENEFIT:

A wholesome and scrumptious is veggie chicken soup. It offers a variety of vitamins and minerals from the veggies in addition to a solid dose of protein from the chicken and beans. It is a robust, filling dish that is ideal for a chilly winter day because of the mix of its ingredients. Also, the recipe's use of olive oil, a source of monounsaturated fats, makes it heart-healthy.

INGREDIENT ALTERNATIVES:

If preferred, you can use tofu or turkey in place of the chicken in this dish. You can also use water or chicken broth in place of the veggie broth. Kale or any leafy green can be used as a substitute if you don't have any spinach on hand. And last, in place of oregano and basil, you can substitute additional spices like cumin, paprika, or chilli powder.

CHICKEN & KALE SOUP

Prep Time: 10 minutes
Cook Time: 15 minutes
Servings: 4-6

INGREDIENTS:

- 2 tablespoons olive oil
- 1 onion, diced
- 2 cloves garlic, minced
- 2 carrots, diced
- 1/2 red bell pepper, diced
- 2 stalks celery, diced
- 1/2 teaspoon dried thyme
- 1/2 teaspoon dried oregano

- 2 bay leaves
- 2 cups chicken stock
- 1/4 teaspoon ground black pepper
- 1/4 teaspoon salt
- 2 cups cooked, shredded chicken
- 2 cups kale, chopped
- 1/2 cup peas (optional)

INSTRUCTIONS:

1. In a big pot over medium heat, warm the olive oil.

2. Include the carrots, bell pepper, celery, onion, and garlic and sauté for 5 minutes, or until the veggies start to soften.

3. Add the bay leaves, thyme, and oregano. Cook for a further minute.

4. Pour in the chicken stock and stir in the black pepper and salt

5. After bringing the mixture to a boil, turn the heat down to low and let it simmer for ten minutes.

6. Add the kale, chicken, and peas, if using, and cook for an additional 5 minutes.

7. Taste and, if necessary, adjust seasoning.

8. Present heat.

NUTRIENT CONTENT (PER SERVING):

220 calories

8g of total fat

2g of saturated fat

39 mg cholesterol

Salt: 473 mg

15g of carbohydrates

3g of fibre

22g of protein

INGREDIENT EXCHANGES:

You can use olive oil or avocado oil in place of olive oil if you want a healthier choice. In addition, you can substitute other veggies for the kale, such as spinach or zucchini. You can use water or vegetable stock in its place if you don't have any chicken stock on hand. And lastly, you can substitute any cooked, shredded meat for the chicken.

ITALIAN TOMATO SOUP

10 minutes to prepare; 4 servings

INGREDIENTS

2 tablespoons of olive oil

1 chopped onion

1 minced garlic clove

1 (14.5 ounces) can of diced tomatoes

1 (14.5 ounce) can of chicken broth

1 teaspoon each of dried oregano and dried basil

1/2 teaspoon sugar

1/4 cup grated Parmesan cheese

2 tablespoons chopped fresh parsley

Instructions

1. Place a big pot on medium heat and heat the olive oil.

2. Add the onion and garlic and sauté for about 5 minutes, or until the onion is soft.

3. Include sugar, salt, pepper, oregano, basil, tomatoes, chicken broth, and sugar. reduce heat, and simmer for 10 minutes.

4. Remove from the heat and toss in the parsley and parmesan cheese.

5. Present heat.

NUTRIENT CONTENT (PER SERVING):

115 calories

7g of fat

2g of saturated fat

5mg of cholesterol

690mg of sodium

9g of carbohydrate

2g of fibre

5g of sugar

4g of protein.

INGREDIENT ALTERNATIVES:

If you don't have any Parmesan cheese, you can use grated Romano or mozzarella cheese. You can substitute dried parsley if you don't have any fresh parsley. For a vegetarian version of this soup, you can use vegetable stock in place of the chicken broth. If you are looking to reduce the sodium content of the soup, you can use low-sodium chicken broth.

MINESTRONE FLORENTINE SOUP

20 minutes for preparation

Time to Cook: 30 minutes

4 servings

INGREDIENTS:

- 2 tablespoons of olive oil

- 2 cloves of garlic, minced

- 2 carrots, diced

- 2 celery stalks, diced

- 2 potatoes, diced

- 1 onion, diced

- 2 tablespoons of tomato paste

- 2 cups of vegetable broth

- 1 can of drained and rinsed, cannellini beans

- 1/2 teaspoon of dried oregano

- 1/2 teaspoon of dried thyme

- 1/4 teaspoon of ground black pepper

- 2 cups of fresh spinach

- 2 tablespoons of chopped fresh parsley

- 2 tablespoons of grated Parmesan cheese

Instructions:

1. In a big pot over medium heat, warm the olive oil.

2. Add the garlic, carrots, celery, potatoes and onions and cook for 10 minutes, stirring occasionally.

3. Add the black pepper, oregano, thyme, tomato paste, vegetable broth, and cannellini beans.

4. Heat to a boil, then lower to a simmer. Cook the vegetables for 20 minutes or until they are soft.

5. Include the spinach and parsley, and cook for a further 5 minutes.

6. Pour the soup into dishes and sprinkle the cheese on top. Serve warm.

NUTRIENT CONTENT (PER SERVING):

216 calories

Fat: 7.2g

1.4g of saturated fat

0 mg of cholesterol

30.3g of carbohydrates

6.3g of fibre

8.7g of protein

Salt: 714 mg

HEALTH BENEFIT:

The beans contribute additional fibre and protein, while the vegetables offer vital vitamins and minerals. The Parmesan cheese and herbs give the dish taste and nutrients.

INGREDIENT ALTERNATIVES:

Other veggies can be included, such as green peppers, green beans, or zucchini, if preferred. Add 1/4 cup of heavy cream or 1/4 cup of plain Greek yoghurt for a creamier texture. For every tablespoon of fresh herbs you don't have, you can use one teaspoon of dried herbs.

VEGETABLE AND BARLEY SOUP

20 minutes for preparation

6 servings

Ingredients:

Extra virgin olive oil, 2 tablespoons (30 ml).

1 big sliced onion

2 minced garlic cloves

2 sliced carrots

2 sliced celery stalks

2 large diced potatoes

1 teaspoon (5 ml) each of dried oregano, thyme, basil, and paprika,

1 teaspoon (5 ml) of each.

One can (14.5 ounces or 411g) of diced tomatoes, undrained;

one cup (150g) of frozen green beans;

one cup (150g) of frozen corn;

two teaspoons (30ml) of fresh parsley, chopped

salt and pepper to taste

INSTRUCTIONS:

1. Heat the olive oil in a large pot over medium heat. Add the onion, garlic, carrots, and celery and cook, stirring occasionally, until the vegetables are tender, about 8 minutes

2. Continue cooking for a further 2 minutes after adding the potatoes, oregano, thyme, basil, and paprika.

3. Add the broth and heat through. Reduce the heat, cover, and simmer for 10 minutes.

4. Add the tomatoes and barley and continue cooking for an additional 10 minutes.

5. Continue cooking for a further 5 minutes after adding the green beans, maize, and parsley.

6. Before serving, season with salt and pepper to taste.

NUTRIENT CONTENT (PER SERVING):

211 calories

4g of total fat

1g of saturated fat

0 mg of cholesterol

37g of carbohydrates

8g of fibre

Sucrose: 6g

7g protein

HEALTH BENEFIT:

This vegetable and barley soup is a wonderful, nutritious low-cholesterol meal. This soup's vegetables are a great source of fibre, vitamins, and minerals. Whole grain barley has been demonstrated to lower cholesterol levels and is high in fibre. This recipe's heart-healthy advantages are further enhanced by the fact that it contains less saturated fat.

INGREDIENT ALTERNATIVES:

Use any other whole grain, such as quinoa, brown rice, or farro, if you don't have pearl barley on hand. Other veggies, including mushrooms, bell peppers, or zucchini, can also be used as a substitute. Fresh tomatoes can be used in place of canned tomatoes if you want. Any frozen vegetable, such as peas or broccoli, may also be used. Last but not least, fresh herbs of any kind can be used in place of dried ones.

CURRIED CAULIFLOWER-LENTIL SOUP

15 minutes for preparation

Time to cook: 30 minutes

8 servings

INGREDIENTS:

- 2 tablespoons (30 ml) vegetable oil
- 1 large onion, chopped
- 2 cloves garlic, minced
- 2 teaspoons (10 ml) curry powder
- 1 teaspoon (5 ml) ground cumin
- 1 teaspoon (5 ml) ground turmeric
- 1/2 teaspoon (2.5 ml) ground coriander
- 1 large cauliflower, cut into florets
- 1 cup (250 ml) washed and drained red lentils

• 2 cups (500 ml) canned diced tomatoes;

• 2 cups (500 ml) vegetable stock

• 1/2 teaspoon (2.5 ml) salt, or to taste

• 1/4 teaspoon (1.25 ml) freshly ground black pepper, or to taste

• 2 tsp each of Freshly chopped cilantro and (30 ml) of freshly squeezed lemon juice

INSTRUCTIONS:

1. Heat the oil in a large pot over medium-high heat. Onion and garlic should be added, and the mixture should boil for three minutes while stirring constantly, or until the onion is soft.

2. Add the curry powder, cumin, turmeric, and coriander, and cook, stirring, for 1 minute.

3. Add the lentils, cauliflower, and vegetable stock and bring them to a boil. The cauliflower and lentils should be soft after 20 minutes of simmering at medium-low heat with occasional stirring.

4. After adding the salt, pepper, and tomatoes, simmer for 5 minutes.

5. Add the cilantro and lemon juice.

6 serve and enjoy!!

NUTRIENT CONTENT (PER SERVING):

149 calories

4.8g of fat

0.6g of saturated fat

20.7g of carbohydrates.

Protein is 6.7g

fiber is 5.7g

cholesterol is 0mg.

595 mg of sodium

SAUSAGE WHITE BEAN STEW

Prep Time: 10 minutes

Cook Time: 25 minutes

Servings: 4-6

INGREDIENTS:

- 1 tablespoon (15ml) olive oil
- 2 cloves garlic, minced
- 1 onion, diced
- 4 links (340g) low-sodium sausage, cut into 1/4 inch thick slices
- 1/2 teaspoon (2.5ml) dried oregano
- 1/2 teaspoon (2.5ml) dried thyme
- 1/2 teaspoon (2.5ml) dried rosemary
- 1/2 teaspoon (2.5ml) ground black pepper
- 2 cups (392g) low-sodium vegetable broth

• 2 (400g) cans white beans, drained and rinsed

• 2 cups (200g) frozen green beans

• 1/2 cup (120ml) dry white wine

• Freshly squeezed lemon juice, 2 tablespoons (30 ml)

• 2 tablespoons (30ml) chopped fresh parsley

INSTRUCTIONS:

1. In a big pot over medium-high heat, warm the olive oil. Add the garlic and onion and cook for 2 minutes, stirring occasionally.

2. Add the pepper, oregano, thyme, rosemary, and sausage chunks. With intermittently stirring, cook for 5 minutes.

3. Add the white beans, green beans, and vegetable broth. Once it has boiled, turn

down the heat, cover, and simmer for 15 minutes.

4. Add lemon juice and white wine. 5 minutes of simmering will be okay.

5. Turn off the heat and add the parsley. Serve hot.

NUTRIENT CONTENT (PER SERVING):

273 calories

Fat: 7.8g

25.2g of carbohydrates

21.2g of protein

16 mg of cholesterol.

Salt: 637 mg

Ingredient Exchanges:

• Lean ground turkey or chicken can be used as a substitute for low-sodium sausage.

• You may use 1 cup (120g) of cooked quinoa and 8 ounces (227g) of mushrooms in place of the sausage if you are vegan or vegetarian.

• Vegetable broth can be used in place of the additional 1/2 cup (120ml) of white wine if you don't have any.

• You can use 2 teaspoons (10ml) of dried parsley as a substitute if you don't have any fresh parsley.

TUSCAN FISH STEW

Prep Time: 30 minutes

Servings: 4

Ingredients:

* 2 tablespoons extra-virgin olive oil

* 1 onion, chopped

* 2 celery stalks, chopped

* 2 cloves garlic, minced

* 1 teaspoon dried oregano

* 2 tablespoons tomato paste

* 4 cups vegetable broth

* 1 large cauliflower head, divided into florets

* 1 (14-ounce) can diced tomatoes

* 1/2 teaspoon sea salt

* 1/4 teaspoon freshly ground black pepper

* 2 (6-ounce) cod fillets, cut into 2-inch pieces
* 2 tablespoons chopped fresh parsley

INSTRUCTIONS:

1. In a big pot over medium heat, warm the olive oil. Cook the onion, celery, and garlic for about 5 minutes, or until the onion is transparent.

2. Cook for another minute after adding the oregano and tomato paste.

3. Bring to a boil the cauliflower, diced tomatoes, vegetable broth, salt, and pepper. For fifteen minutes, simmer over low heat.

4. Include the cod and cook for a further 5 minutes, or until the fish is fully cooked.

5. Pour the stew into bowls and sprinkle the parsley on top. Serve warm.

NUTRIENT CONTENT (PER SERVING):

228 calories

Fat: 11.3g

16.2g of carbohydrates

16.9g of protein

5.0g of fibre

NaCl: 578 mg

HEALTH BENEFIT:

A terrific recipe that is low in cholesterol is this Tuscan Fish Stew. The primary ingredients of fish and veggies are good providers of lean protein and nutritional fibre, and all of the ingredients are low in cholesterol. Moreover, vegetables supply important vitamins and minerals. The tomato paste offers a good amount of lycopene, and the olive oil is a fantastic source of beneficial fats. This stew is a fantastic method to acquire your recommended daily allowance of nourishment while regulating your cholesterol levels.

INGREDIENT ALTERNATIVES:

Haddock, halibut, or tilapia are all acceptable alternatives to cod fillets if you don't have any on hand. You can eliminate the parsley altogether if you don't have any fresh, or you can use dried parsley instead. Garlic powder can be used in its place if fresh garlic is unavailable. You can substitute water or chicken broth if you don't have any veggie broth on hand. You can use any other vegetable, such as broccoli, carrots, or mushrooms, in place of cauliflower.

CREAMY MUSHROOM AND KALE SOUP

20 minutes for preparation

4 servings

INGREDIENTS:

Olive oil, 3 tablespoons

1 diced onion

2 minced garlic cloves

500g diced mushrooms

1 teaspoon of thyme leaves, fresh

2 tablespoons of regular flour

two cups of vegetable broth

Cream 200 ml

1 cup chopped kale

To taste, add salt and pepper.

INSTRUCTIONS:

1. In a big pot over medium-high heat, warm the olive oil.

2. Add the onion and garlic and simmer for about 5 minutes, or until tender.

3. Include the mushrooms and thyme, and simmer for 10 minutes, or until the mushrooms are tender and the liquid has evaporated.

4. Add the flour and blend by stirring.

5. Add the cream and vegetable stock and bring to a boil.

6. Lower the heat, then simmer the food for 10 minutes.

7. Add the kale and cook for a further 5 minutes.

8. To taste, add salt and pepper to the dish.

9. Present heat. Enjoy!

NUTRIENT CONTENT (PER SERVING):

Energy: 287 kcal

16.3 g of carbohydrates.

6.9 g of protein

Fat: 22.4 g

8.0 g of saturated fat

41 mg cholesterol

Salt: 637 mg

1.7 g of fibre

INGREDIENT ALTERNATIVES:

Half-and-half, whole milk, or even plain Greek yoghurt can be used in place of cream if you don't have any on hand. You can substitute oregano or other herbs of your choice if you don't have the thyme. You can skip the cream and substitute veggie stock for the chicken stock if you prefer a vegan version. You can use gluten-free flour to make a version without gluten.

LENTIL AND TOMATO STEW

Prep Time: 15 minutes

4 servings

INGREDIENTS:

Olive oil, 2 tablespoons

1 chopped onion

2 chopped garlic cloves -

 2 diced carrots

1 diced celery stalk

Paprika, 1 teaspoon

2 cups vegetable stock

1 teaspoon cumin powder

Red lentils, 2 cups

2 cans of diced tomatoes, each 14.5 ounces

 Tomato paste, 2 teaspoons

two teaspoons of red wine vinegar

two tablespoons of freshly chopped parsley

To taste, salt and pepper

INSTRUCTIONS:

1. In a big pot over medium-high heat, warm the olive oil. Cook the carrots, celery, onion, and garlic for 5 minutes, or until tender.

2. Add the cumin and paprika and blend.

3. Add the red wine vinegar, parsley, tomatoes, lentils, tomato paste, and vegetable stock. Bring to a boil, reduce the heat to a simmer, and cook for 15 minutes.

4. To taste, add salt and pepper to the dish.

NUTRIENT CONTENT (PER SERVING):

302 calories

Fat: 5g

45g of carbohydrates

13g of protein

6g of fibre

565 mg of sodium

INGREDIENT ALTERNATIVES:

- Vegetable or canola oil may be substituted for olive oil.

- You can substitute oregano or thyme for paprika or cumin if you don't have either.

- Vegetable broth can be used in place of vegetable stock.

- You are free to use any variety of lentils, including green, black, or brown ones.

- You can use dried parsley in place of fresh if you don't have any.

- You can use balsamic vinegar or apple cider vinegar if you don't have red wine vinegar.

VEGETABLE BARLEY STEW

Prep Time: 15 minutes

Cook Time: 60 minutes

Servings: 4

INGREDIENTS:

- 1 tablespoon of vegetable oil
- 1 onion, diced
- 2 cloves garlic, minced
- 2 celery stalks, diced
- 2 carrots, peeled and diced
- 2 cups pearl barley, uncooked
- 2 tablespoons tomato paste
- 5 cups vegetable stock
- 2 bay leaves
- 2 tablespoons fresh parsley, chopped
- 1 teaspoon dried oregano

- 1 teaspoon dried thyme

- 1/2 teaspoon sea salt

- 1/4 teaspoon freshly ground black pepper

- 2 cups of mixed vegetables such as green beans, peas, corn, etc.

INSTRUCTIONS:

1. Heat the oil in a large pot over medium-high heat.

2. Add the onion and garlic and sauté for about 5 minutes, or until tender.

3. Add the celery and carrots and continue to sauté for a further 3 minutes.

4. Add the tomato paste and barley and mix to incorporate.

5. Pour in the vegetable stock and add the bay leaves, parsley, oregano, thyme, salt, and pepper. Stir to combine.

6. Bring the mixture to a boil, then lower the heat to a simmer, stirring regularly, for 45 minutes.

7. Add the mixed veggies and simmer for a further 15 minutes, or until the vegetables are fully cooked and the barley is soft.

8. Remove from the heat and discard the bay leaves. Taste and adjust the seasoning if necessary.

NUTRIENT CONTENT (PER SERVING):

• 295 calories

Sodium: 717 mg

5.1g of fat

0.6g of saturated fat.

51.3g of carbohydrates

12.3g of fibre

8.4g of protein

INGREDIENT ALTERNATIVES:

• Quinoa or brown rice can be used as a substitute if you don't have pearl barley.

• Beef or chicken stock can be used in place of vegetable stock.

• Dried herbs can be used in place of fresh herbs if you don't have any on hand.

• You may also use whatever other vegetables you have on hand in place of the mixed vegetables.

VEGETABLES AND VEGAN

VEGETABLES AND VEGAN

THAI SOBA NOODLES WITH SPRING VEGGIES

15 minutes for preparation; 2 servings

INGREDIENTS:

- Sesame oil, 2 tablespoons (30 ml).
- 1/2 cup (50 g) of thinly sliced red onion
- 1/2 cup (50 g) of julienned carrots
- 100 grammes or 1 cup of sugar snap peas
- 2 minced garlic cloves
- 5 grammes of freshly grated ginger, 1 tsp
- Soy sauce, 2 tablespoons (30 ml).
- Rice vinegar, 2 tablespoons (30 ml).
- Honey, 2 teaspoons (30 ml)
- Red pepper flakes, 1/2 teaspoon (2.5 g)
- Two packages of soba noodles
- 2 teaspoons of lime juice, fresh (30 ml)

• Two tablespoons (30 ml) of freshly chopped cilantro

• Two teaspoons (twenty ml) of freshly chopped basil

INSTRUCTIONS:

1 Heat a large skillet or wok over medium heat.

2. Add the sugar snap peas, red onion, carrots, and sesame oil. Simmer for about 5 minutes, stirring frequently, or until the vegetables are tender.

3. Add the ginger and garlic, and simmer for approximately a minute, or until fragrant.

4. Add the red pepper flakes, rice vinegar, honey, and soy sauce. To blend, stir.

5. Add the soba noodles and simmer for about 5 minutes, or until they are soft.

6. Turn off the heat and whisk in the basil, cilantro, and lime juice.

7. Split the noodles between two plates and serve.

NUTRIENT CONTENT (PER SERVING):

Carbohydrates: 53 g

Fiber: 5 g

Sugar: 12 g

Protein: 8 g

Calories: 342

Cholesterol: 0 mg;

Sodium: 677 mg.

INGREDIENT ALTERNATIVES:

Yellow onion can be used in place of red onion if it's not available. You can substitute any fresh vegetable, such as broccoli, bell peppers, or mushrooms if you don't have sugar snap peas. Dried herbs can be used in place of fresh cilantro and basil if necessary. You can swap the honey for maple syrup if you're looking for a vegan option. If you don't have soba noodles, you can also substitute udon, spaghetti, or linguine for the dish.

VEGAN RATATOUILLE

20 minutes for preparation

4 servings

INGREDIENTS:

- 2 tablespoons of olive oil

- 1 diced red onion

- 2 minced garlic cloves

- 1 large red pepper

- 2 diced zucchini

- 2 diced eggplant

- One can of diced tomatoes

- 1/4 teaspoon of red pepper flakes

- 1 teaspoon each of dried oregano and basil

- 2 teaspoons finely chopped fresh parsley

- Salt and pepper to taste

INSTRUCTIONS:

1. In a big skillet over medium heat, warm the olive oil.

2. Add the red onion and garlic, and cook for 3-4 minutes, stirring occasionally.

3. Stirring occasionally, sauté the red pepper, zucchini, and eggplant for 5-7 minutes.

4. Add the chopped tomatoes, oregano, basil, red pepper flakes, and parsley, and cook for an additional 5-7 minutes, stirring occasionally.

5. To Taste add salt and pepper.

6. Present hot.

NUTRIENT CONTENT (PER SERVING):

123 calories

Fat: 5g

19g of carbohydrates

3g. protein

5g of fibre

Salt: 127 mg

Ingredient Exchanges:

- Other vegetable oils, including olive oil or avocado oil, can be used in place of olive oil.

- White or yellow onions can be used in place of red onions.

- Green, yellow, or orange bell peppers can be used in place of red bell pepper.

- Butternut squash or summer squash can be used in place of zucchini.

- You can use cauliflower or mushrooms in place of the eggplant.

- Instead of dry oregano, use fresh oregano.

- You can use fresh basil for dry basil.

- Fresh basil or cilantro can be used in place of fresh parsley.

LENTIL BOLOGNESE

Prep Time: 15 minutes

Servings: 4

INGREDIENTS:

- 2 tablespoons olive oil
- 2 cloves of garlic, minced
- 1 onion, diced
- 2 carrots, diced
- 2 stalks of celery, diced
- 2 tablespoons tomato paste
- 2 cups of cooked lentils
- 2 cups of vegetable stock
- 2 teaspoons of dried oregano
- 2 tablespoons of red wine vinegar
- 2 tablespoons of nutritional yeast
- Salt and pepper to taste

• 1/2 cup of chopped fresh parsley

INSTRUCTIONS:

1. In a big pot over medium heat, warm the olive oil.

2. Include the vegetables and sauté for 3 to 5 minutes, or until the vegetables are tender.

3. Add the tomato paste and blend by stirring.

4. Bring to a boil after adding the cooked lentils, vegetable stock, oregano, red wine vinegar, and nutritional yeast.

5. Reduce the heat to low and simmer for 10-15 minutes until the sauce has thickened and the lentils are cooked through.

6. Add pepper and salt to taste.

7. Add the chopped parsley and serve the pasta of your choice.

NUTRIENT CONTENT (PER SERVING):

290 calories

Fat: 7 g

1 g of saturated fat

0 mg of cholesterol

Salt: 150 mg

42 g of carbohydrates

9 g of fibre

Sucrose: 6 g

14 g of protein

NUTRIENT CONTENT (PER SERVING):

• Balsamic or apple cider vinegar can be substituted for red wine vinegar if you don't have any.

• You can substitute grated Parmesan cheese for nutritional yeast if you don't have any on hand.

• Fresh basil or oregano can be substituted for fresh parsley if you don't have any on hand.

SPICY PINTO BEAN QUINOA BOWL

20 minutes for preparation

4 servings

INGREDIENTS:

- 1/2 cup rinsed and drained quinoa (90g)
- One small onion, diced
- one teaspoon (5 ml) of olive oil (45g)
- 2 minced garlic cloves
- 1 teaspoon chilli powder (5ml),
- 1/2 teaspoon smoked paprika
- 1/2 teaspoon ground cumin (2.5ml)
- Two cups of veggie broth (480ml)
- 1 can of washed and drained pinto beans (400g)
- 1 cup corn, frozen (150g)

• Green chillies, 2 tablespoons diced (30 ml)

• fresh cilantro, 2 teaspoons chopped (30ml)

• Add salt and freshly ground black pepper to taste.

INSTRUCTIONS:

1. Heat the oil in a large pot over medium heat. Add the onion and cook until softened, about 5 minutes.

2. Add the garlic, cumin, chili powder, and smoked paprika and cook for 1 minute until fragrant.

3. Add the broth and quinoa, and then heat to a boil. Lower heat to medium and let the quinoa simmer for 15 minutes, covered, or until fully cooked.

4. Continue cooking for a further 5 minutes after adding the pinto beans, corn, and green chillies.

5. Stir in the cilantro after removing it from the heat. Add salt and pepper to the meal to taste.

6. Present hot.

NUTRIENT CONTENT (PER SERVING):

258 calories

9.4g of protein

Fat: 4.1g

42.2g of carbohydrates

7.2g of fibre

Salt: 413 mg

INGREDIENT ALTERNATIVES:

You can use dried cilantro if you don't have any fresh. Black beans or kidney beans can alternatively be used in place of pinto beans. You can substitute water for vegetable broth if you don't have any. Last but not least, you can use red pepper flakes or a dash of cayenne pepper if you don't have chilli powder.

Jeffery F. Maurer

TOFU AND ROOT VEGETABLE CURRY

15 minutes for preparation

forty-five minutes to cook

4 servings

INGREDIENTS:

Olive oil, 2 tablespoons

- 1 finely chopped onion

- 2 minced garlic cloves

- 1 teaspoon of coriander, ground

- 1 teaspoon cumin, ground

- One tablespoon of ground turmeric

Garam masala, 1 teaspoon

- 1/2 teaspoon ginger, ground

- 1/2 teaspoon cinnamon, ground

- 2 chopped and peeled carrots

- 2 diced and peeled potatoes

- 1 sweet potato, diced after being peeled

2-cups of vegetable broth

- Diced tomatoes, 1 can (14.5 ounces)

- Coconut milk, 14.5 ounces in a can.

- One box (14 ounces) of diced extra-firm tofu

-2 teaspoons lime juice that has just been squeezed

¼ cup of freshly chopped cilantro

INSTRUCTIONS:

1. Heat the oil in a large pot over medium heat.

2. Add the onion and garlic and simmer, stirring regularly, for about 5 minutes, or until the onion is tender.

3. Add the coriander, cumin, turmeric, garam masala, ginger, and cinnamon and cook, stirring frequently, until fragrant, about 1 minute.

4. Add the carrots, potatoes, and sweet potatoes and simmer, stirring often, for about 5 minutes, or until the veggies start to soften.

5. Add the tomatoes, coconut milk, and vegetable broth and bring to a boil.

6. Lower the heat to a low simmer and cook the vegetables for about 25 minutes, stirring occasionally.

7. Include the tofu and boil for about 5 minutes, or until heated completely.

8. Add the cilantro and lime juice.

9. Serve the curry hot.

NUTRIENT CONTENT (PER SERVING):

Energy: 272 kcal

33 g of carbohydrates

13 g of protein

Fat: 11 g

5.7 g of saturated fat

0 mg of cholesterol

Salt: 559 mg

5.6 g of fibre

HEALTH BENEFIT:

Due to its high protein and dietary fibre content, this tofu and root vegetable curry is a fantastic option for those trying to lower their cholesterol. This curry is a filling, nutrient-rich dish thanks to the mixture of veggies, spices, and tofu. Coconut milk and lime juice are added, which enhances the flavour and helps to balance the spices.

NUTRIENT CONTENT (PER SERVING):

Feel free to omit or substitute any of the components if you don't have them all. For instance, you can substitute normal potatoes if you don't have any sweet potatoes. Other veggies, including bell peppers, zucchini, or eggplant, can also be used in their place. You can substitute mild coconut milk or even almond milk if you don't have any coconut milk on hand. Try adding a cup of cooked quinoa or a can of chickpeas for a different flavour.

Jeffery F. Maurer

Jeffery F. Maurer

SOUTHWESTERN MILLET-STUFFED TOMATOES

30 minutes for preparation

4 servings

INGREDIENTS:

4 large tomatoes

1/2 cup millet

1 teaspoon olive oil

1 teaspoon each of chopped onion, bell pepper, and zucchini

1/2 cup cooked black beans

1 teaspoon each of chilli powder and cumin

1/4 teaspoon of garlic powder.

Add salt and pepper to taste

Add half a cup of cheddar cheese, shredded.

INSTRUCTIONS:

1. Set the oven temperature to 375°F (190°C).

2. Cut each tomato's top off, scoop out the insides, and save the tops. The tomatoes should be put in a baking dish.

3. Prepare the millet as directed on the packet.

4. In a big skillet over medium heat, warm the olive oil. Add the onion, bell pepper, and zucchini and cook for 5 minutes, or until the vegetables are tender.

5. Add the black beans, cumin, chilli powder, garlic powder, salt, and cooked millet. Cook for a further five minutes, stirring now and then.

6. Place a millet mixture inside each tomato and top with the reserved tomato tops. Sprinkle with the cheese.

7. Bake for 20 minutes, or until the tomatoes are soft and the cheese has melted.

NUTRIENT CONTENT (PER SERVING):

226 calories

Fat: 8.4g

29.8g of carbohydrates

6.3g of fibre

9.3g of protein

BROWN RICE AND SWEET POTATO PILAF

25 minutes for preparation

4 servings

INGREDIENTS:

2 tablespoons of olive oil

2 cloves of minced garlic

1 large onion, coarsely diced

1 sweet potato that has been peeled and chopped.

2 cups of brown rice

4 cups of vegetable broth.

1 teaspoon of dried thyme and dry oregano.

INSTRUCTIONS:

1. In a big pot set over medium heat, warm the olive oil.

2. Add the onion and garlic and simmer for about 5 minutes, or until tender.

3. Add the brown rice and stir for 1 minute.

4. Add the sweet potato, oregano, thyme, vegetable broth, salt, and pepper. up to a boil.

5. Lower the heat to low, cover the pan, and simmer the rice for 20 minutes, or until it is tender.

6. Present hot.

NUTRIENT CONTENT (PER SERVING):

330 calories

Fat: 8g

53g of carbohydrates

8g protein

5g of fibre

Salt: 498 mg

CHILI-SAUTÉED TOFU WITH ALMONDS

Prep Time: 10 minutes | Servings: 4

INGREDIENTS:

• 500g extra firm tofu, drained and cut into cubes

• 2 tablespoons olive oil

• 2 cloves garlic, minced

• 1 teaspoon ground cumin

• 1 teaspoon dried oregano

• 1 teaspoon chili powder

• ¼ teaspoon sea salt

• ¼ teaspoon ground black pepper

• 2 tablespoons tamari or soy sauce

• 2 tablespoons almond butter

• 2 tablespoons agave syrup

- 2 tablespoons freshly squeezed lime juice
- 2 tablespoons chopped fresh cilantro
- ¼ cup sliced almonds

INSTRUCTIONS:

1. In a big skillet over medium heat, warm the oil.

2. Add the garlic and sauté for 1 minute.

3. Add the tofu cubes and cook for about 5 minutes, or until golden brown.

4. Add the cumin, oregano, chili powder, salt, and pepper and cook for 1 minute.

.5. Cook for 2 minutes after adding the tamari, almond butter, agave syrup, and lime juice.

6. Turn off the heat and stir in the almonds and cilantro.

7. Present hot.

NUTRIENT CONTENT (PER SERVING):

192 calories,

11.3g of fat,

14.1g of carbohydrates

11.2g of protein,

320mg of sodium

3.3g of fibre.

TOFU WITH CHIMICHURRI SAUCE

Prep Time: 15 minutes

Servings: 4

INGREDIENTS:

400 grammes of firm tofu, cubed and drained

2 tablespoons of olive oil

2 minced garlic cloves

Finely cut the

2 tablespoons of fresh parsley

2 tablespoons of fresh oregano

2 tablespoons of fresh basil,

2 tablespoons of red wine vinegar

1/4 teaspoon of red pepper flakes

2 tablespoons of extra-virgin olive oil.

- To taste, salt and pepper

INSTRUCTIONS:

1. Set the oven to 400°F (200°C).

2. Spoon some olive oil over the cubed tofu in a small baking tray.

3. Bake for 15 minutes, or until the food is cooked through and has a light golden colour.

4. In the meantime, combine the extra virgin olive oil, red wine vinegar, garlic, parsley, oregano, basil, salt, and pepper in a small bowl. Combine everything thoroughly.

5. After the tofu has cooked through, take it out of the oven and place it on a serving tray.

6. Add the chimichurri sauce on top and dish up.

NUTRIENT CONTENT (PER SERVING):

179 calories

5.7g of carbohydrates

11.5g of protein

Fat: 13.8g

2g of saturated fat

0 mg of cholesterol

Salt: 133 mg

1.7g of fibre

MEAT RECIPES

MEAT DISHES

Jeffery F. Maurer

MEATBALL LINGUINE

Preparation: one hour

4-6 servings

INGREDIENTS:

2 eggs

2 minced garlic cloves

2 tablespoons of chopped fresh parsley

2 tablespoons of grated parmesan cheese

2 tablespoons of breadcrumbs

500g of linguine

500g of lean ground beef -

2 tablespoons of extra virgin olive oil

1 teaspoon of dried oregano

1/2 teaspoon of salt

1/4 teaspoon of ground black pepper

2 cans of chopped tomatoes (400g each)

INSTRUCTIONS:

1. Set the oven's temperature to 350°F (175°C).

2. Combine the breadcrumbs, oregano, salt, pepper, parsley, eggs, garlic, Parmesan cheese, and ground beef in a sizable bowl.

3. Create little meatballs out of the mixture (about 1 inch in diameter).

4. Arrange the meatballs on a parchment-lined baking pan.

5. Bake the meatballs in the preheated oven for 15-20 minutes, or until they are thoroughly cooked.

6. Meanwhile, bring a large pot of salted water to a boil. Add the linguine and cook according to package instructions.

7. Heat the olive oil in a large skillet over medium-high heat.

8. Add the chopped tomatoes and simmer for 5 minutes while stirring occasionally.

9. Stir in the prepared meatballs and simmer for a further five minutes.

10. Drain the cooked linguine and add it to the skillet with the meatballs and tomatoes.

11. Simmer for five minutes while occasionally stirring.

12. Present the hot meatball linguine.

NUTRIENT CONTENT (PER SERVING):

380 calories

Fat: 13g

24g of protein

38g of carbohydrates

4g of fibre

Salt: 700 mg

90 mg cholesterol

PORK SKEWERS

15 minutes for preparation

4 servings

INGREDIENTS:

500g of trimmed and cubed pork fillet

2 tablespoons of olive oil

2 cloves of finely minced garlic

2 tablespoons of lemon juice

1 teaspoon each of dried oregano and ground cumin

2 tablespoons each of freshly chopped parsley and coriande

salt and freshly ground black pepper to taste

8 wooden skewers (soaked in water for 30 minutes before use)

INSTRUCTIONS:

1. Preheat the grill or barbecue.

2. In a large bowl, combine the pork cubes, olive oil, garlic, lemon juice, oregano, cumin, parsley, coriander, salt and pepper. To mingle, stir.

3. Arrange the pieces of onion and bell pepper in between the pork cubes on the wooden skewers, if you like.

4. Place the skewers on the preheated grill or barbecue and cook for 10 minutes, turning occasionally, until the pork is cooked through.

5. Serve the pork skewers with a green salad.

Jeffery F. Maurer

NUTRIENT CONTENT (PER SERVING):

- 250 calories
- 11.5g of fat; 2.5g of saturated fat; 70 mg of cholesterol
- 85 mg of sodium

Protein: 28g;

Fiber: 0.5g

Carbohydrates: 2.5g

DIJON SIRLOIN STEAK

4 servings

10 minutes for preparation

Time to Cook: 10 minutes

NUTRIENT CONTENT (PER SERVING):

Energy: 257 kcal

2.6 g of carbohydrates

Fat: 10.9 g

33.7 g of protein

75 mg cholesterol

Salt: 462 mg

INGREDIENTS:

1 pound of sirloin steak, divided into 4 steaks

2 tablespoons of Dijon mustard

1 teaspoon each of garlic and onion powder

1/4 teaspoon of black pepper

1 tablespoon of olive oil

2 tablespoons of butter

2 tablespoons of freshly chopped parsley

2 tablespoons of freshly chopped chives.

INSTRUCTIONS:

1. Set the oven's temperature to 375 degrees Fahrenheit.

2. Arrange the steaks on a baking sheet and sprinkle black pepper, garlic powder, and onion powder on both sides of each piece.

3. Heat the olive oil in a large skillet over medium-high heat.

4. Add the steaks to the heated skillet and cook for 4 minutes on each side.

5. Take out the steaks and set them on the baking sheet from the skillet.

6. Add butter on top of each steak after dousing it in Dijon mustard.

7. Bake in the preheated oven for 6 to 8 minutes, depending on how done you like your steaks.

8. Take the steaks out of the oven and give them five minutes to cool before serving.

9. Garnish with fresh parsley and chives before serving.

INGREDIENT ALTERNATIVES:

• Tenderloin or top round are two lean beef cuts that can be used in place of the sirloin steak.

• Low-sodium mustard or a vinaigrette made in the style of Dijon can be used in place of the Dijon mustard.

• Fresh garlic and onion can be used in place of the garlic and onion powder.

• Canola or avocado oil can be used in place of olive oil.

• You can use margarine or a vegan butter alternative in place of the butter.

• You can use dried herbs like basil, oregano, or thyme in place of fresh herbs.

SUN-DRIED TOMATO CHOPS

10 minutes for preparation

4 servings

INGREDIENTS:

- 4 Boneless Pork Loin chops (500g)

- 2 tablespoons of olive oil

- 2 cloves of garlic, finely chopped

- 1 teaspoon of dried oregano

- 3 tablespoons of sun-dried tomatoes, finely chopped

- 2 tablespoons of fresh parsley, finely chopped

- 2 tablespoons of white wine

- 1 tablespoon of balsamic vinegar

- Salt and freshly ground black pepper to taste

NUTRIENT CONTENT (PER SERVING):

kilocalories: 200

Fat total: 10.3g

2.4g of saturated fat

62mg of cholesterol

Salt: 83.3 mg

2.6g of total carbohydrates

0.8g of dietary fibre

20.9g of protein

Instructions:

1. Set the oven's thermostat to 180 C (350 F).

2. Place the pork chops in a shallow baking dish and rub them with the olive oil. Sprinkle with the garlic, oregano, sun-dried tomatoes,

parsley, white wine, and balsamic vinegar. Season with salt and pepper to taste.

3. Bake the pork chops in the preheated oven for about 30 minutes, or until they are fully done.

4. Present the chops of sun-dried tomato hot.

Jeffery F. Maurer

GRILLED TURKEY AND VEGGIE KABOBS

4 servings

15 minutes for preparation

20 minutes for cooking

INGREDIENTS:

500 grammes of cubed lean turkey breast

1 red bell pepper

2 green pepper

1 red onion

2 zucchini, 1-inch slices;

2 tablespoons of olive oil

2 teaspoons of garlic powder

1 teaspoon of smoked paprika

1/2 teaspoon of cumin

1/2 teaspoon of black pepper

2 tablespoons of lemon juice

1 tablespoon of chopped fresh thyme.

INSTRUCTIONS:

1. Preheat the grill to medium-high heat.

2. Combine cubed turkey, bell peppers, onion, zucchini, olive oil, ground cumin, black pepper, lemon juice, and fresh thyme in a big bowl. Stir everything together until it's all distributed equally.

3. Using metal skewers, thread turkey and vegetables onto skewers, alternating between meat and vegetables.

4. Use cooking spray or oil to grease the grill grates. Kabobs should be placed on the grill

and cooked for 8 to 10 minutes, flipping them to ensure equal cooking.

5. Turn the heat off and allow the food to cool before serving.

NUTRIENT CONTENT (PER SERVING):

172 calories

Fat: 7.9 g

Protein: 20.6 g Carbohydrates: 7.2 g

42 mg of cholesterol

Salt: 108 mg

LEMON TARRAGON TURKEY MEDALLIONS

10 minutes for preparation

Time to Cook: 15 minutes

4 servings

Ingredients:

- Four (4-ounce) turkey medallions

- two teaspoons each of olive oil, Dijon mustard, and chopped fresh tarragon.

- Freshly squeezed lemon juice, 2 tablespoons

– One teaspoon of garlic powder

- To taste, sea salt and freshly ground black pepper

Instructions:

1 Start by setting the oven to 375°F (190°C).

2. Arrange the turkey medallions on a parchment-lined baking pan.

3. Combine olive oil, Dijon mustard, tarragon, lemon juice, and garlic powder in a small bowl.

4. Pour the mixture over the turkey medallions and season with salt and pepper

5. Bake the turkey for 15 minutes, or until it is thoroughly done.

NUTRIENT CONTENT (PER SERVING):

Energy: 189 kcal

0.5 g of carbohydrates

Fat: 8.3 g Protein: 26.3 g

1.3 g of saturated fat

56 mg cholesterol

200 mg. of sodium

0.3 g of fibre

BALSAMIC ROSEMARY CHICKEN

4 servings

10 minutes for preparation

Time to Cook: 25 minutes

Ingredients:

- 4 skinless, boneless breasts of chicken

-2 tsp. extra virgin olive oil

- 2 minced garlic cloves

- 2 teaspoons minced fresh rosemary

- 2 tablespoons honey - 2 teaspoons balsamic vinegar

- To taste, salt and pepper

INSTRUCTIONS:

1 Start by setting the oven to 375°F (190°C).

2. Put chicken breasts in an oven-safe dish.

3. Combine olive oil, garlic, rosemary, balsamic vinegar, honey, salt, and pepper in a small bowl.

4. Pour the mixture over the chicken breasts and turn to coat.

5. Bake for 25 minutes in a preheated oven, or until chicken is thoroughly cooked and juices are clear.

6. Present hot.

NUTRIENT CONTENT (PER SERVING):

Energy: 315 kcal

Fat total: 11.3 g

2.3 g of saturated fat

83 mg of cholesterol

Salt: 156 mg

17.7 g of total carbohydrates

0.2 g of dietary fibre

16.4 g of sugars

32.2 g of protein

Jeffery F. Maurer

Dear valued reader,

Thank you for reading and trying out our recipes. We hope you enjoyed them and found them useful. Please take a moment to drop a review in the comments section of this cookbook. Your feedback is greatly appreciated! Your honest reviews will help me continue creating more great recipes and help us increase our improvement.

Thank you once again.

Follow Jeffery F. Maurer where She shares Free recipes on Daily at Her online page and Also Reach Out to Her if You Have any questions:

Email: jefferyf.maurer@gmail.com

Instagram: Jeffery F. Maurer

BONUS

A. She Also Gives out Free Food and Shopping List Journals Which you can Print out and use.

B. Also get here Anti inflammatory diets cookbook, message Her via email for instant access.

To get this message Her with

Jeffery F. Maurer

"I Need Your Food and shopping list Journal" Via Email.